As you read Eddie's compelling story, you see a child starting out with such potential, then rejected, ever more disillusioned and embittered with his lot, drift into the dark-side of life and into a adult life of crime and realise that only a power greater than himself could see the positives in this tough personality and transform it to help others.

When Eddie came to breaking point, committed Christians encouraged him to change, to become part of a church and to start to use his experiences to help others.

This is a book that gives hope and could change lives.

Paul Cowley, Director
Alpha for Prisons
Caring for Ex-Offenders

Eddie Murison's story is one that shows that no matter how far a man goes down into the mire of sin, addiction and depravity the Lord can begin a work in that life. The heavenly artist does not give up, but continues to chip away with the hammer of love and the chisel of grace, and eventually out of the marred and damaged mess comes one of God's masterpieces. '

Canon Noel Proctor

Former Chapl

D0434494

If Satan the Accuser has been whispering in your ear
You just tell him you're forgiven—
He's got no business here.
'Cos it doesn't matter what you've done,
It matters what you'll be.
There is no condemnation where the Son has set you free.

Don Francisco

TO THE XTREME

THE EDDIE MURISON STORY
ANNE SUTHERLAND
& EDDIE MURISON

CHRISTIAN FOCUS

Copyright © Anne Sutherland and Eddie Murison 2005

10 9 8 7 6 5 4 3 2 1

ISBN 1-84550-078-4

Eddie's story was previously told in
Bruised but not Broken (ISBN 1-87592-113-5)
written with Betty McKay and published in 1994.

First published in 2005
by
Christian Focus Publications,
Geanies House, Fearn, Ross-shire,
IV20 1TW, Scotland.

www.christianfocus.com

Cover design by Alister MacInnes

Printed and bound by
Nørhaven Paperback A/S, Denmark

Contents

Dedication

For...
- the friends who invested so much in my life and to whom I would not be where I am today.

- my late mother Muriel whom I miss, but will one day meet again in heaven.

- those who love the unlovable, are committed to the uncommitted, respond to the unresponsive and who give to the faithless, give hope to the hopeless and give time to the lonely

And most of all...
- to my beautiful wife Leslie, who has been far more then a wife to me. You are

my best friend. Thank you for being my strength and pushing me on. Thank you for the lovely children you gave me.

- To Fiona, Heather and Stuart – You are all a blessing from God to me and I thank him each day for you.

Introduction

'I've got a job for you to do. I want to do a follow-up' said Eddie confidently 'and I thought you might like to write it for me'. I want to go beyond the big story of how I became a Christian and tell people that it isn't easy. I need to tell people some of the lessons I've learned. I want to make sure that people know it's not 'happy ever after...'

'Tell me about it' I said.

Now several years on, *Bruised Not Broken* (Eddie's 'big story') is out of print and *To the Xtreme*, whilst incorporating a shortened version of his 'big story', brings readers up-to-date and tells the very down-to-earth story that followed.

Eddie, his wife Leslie and I met in Perth whilst Eddie was working for Prison Fellowship Scotland. As I got to know them better it became increasingly clear how different our backgrounds were. Whilst I had a sheltered, stable, almost idyllic country upbringing Eddie's was the total opposite — rejected as a child, a rebellious and angry youth who turned into a violent and dangerous criminal. We surely had little in common?

But I recognised the road he was on. It is the same road that all Christians find themselves travelling. We all start out in the city of Self Destruct and we all walk the road towards the Celestial City together — travellers from every part of life, rich and poor, slave and free, black and white. Our experiences on the road are all different but this story illustrates that many of the lessons are the same.

Eddie's early life was very 'ugly' but this story is about how his life has been made beautiful. Eddie needed to change. But first and foremost he needed a Saviour. And when he found forgiveness through the Lord Jesus Christ not only did it profoundly change him but God gave him a new will to change… and he worked hard to change…

'What I am is a message of hope for you guys and the evidence that your lives can change too' says Eddie. It is our prayer that many will find that sure and certain hope.

Anne Sutherland

Part One:
Bruised not Broken

1. Rejected Boy

'When Fear Slowly Hardens to Hate'

'What's he want? We dinna want him here.' Not many words, but the man's tone of voice was enough. Eddie's whole life would be shaped by the terrible knowledge that he was a reject. Not wanted.

His Granda had lived in a tall granite tenement block on the middle floor of number eighteen. Granda, Jim Murison, was originally from Peterhead but when his wife died, he and his eight surviving children – four boys and four girls – moved to this three bedroomed tenement in Aberdeen.

At home Eddie's grandfather was a strict man and did his best to see that none of his family got into trouble – with the law or in any other way. His daughter Muriel (Eddie's mother), as a late teenager, found some of his restrictions annoying—especially his ban on going out with boys. She must have found more than a few illicit moments of freedom because she was barely out of her teens when Eddie made his appearance.

Jim Murison's reaction is not recorded, but he allowed his daughter to live on at home and from then on he was 'Granda' to Eddie. When Eddie's mum found a new boyfriend, Granda didn't like him. Many a time he advised his daughter to have nothing to do with the lad. But she was as headstrong as he and when the wedding went ahead Eddie was taken to live in his stepfather's house, away from his beloved Granda.

Eddie's whole life seemed to be haunted by fear in those early years. And underlying everything was the fear of his stepfather, a fear which was slowly hardening into hatred. Eddie felt rejection in his every glance.

Nor was the man's resentment confined to glances—violence was never far below the surface. He would pick on the least misdeed and punish Eddie, and if his Mum butted in to help, she would get it too. The angry man would pin his wife against a wall: 'That basket doesna' belong here!' he would shout. And there would be blows, first for his wife and then for Eddie.

When Eddie was nine years old the family moved north. For Eddie this meant another new school, amongst complete strangers. He found it hard to settle, especially when the teacher made him stand in a corner for some minor misdeed. He felt such a fool. Eddie decided to get his own back.

That weekend he broke into the school, went to his classroom and tore up all the jotters and exercise books he could find. Then he set fire to them. It was quite a blaze. In fact he began to get a bit worried so he grabbed the fire extinguisher and sprayed it around wildly, leaving tell-tale footprints in the foam!

When the damage was discovered on Monday morning, the police were called in and the prints gave Eddie away. It was his first brush with the law.

This incident did nothing to ease the constant tension at home. Fear and anger and the constantly rubbed–in rejection grew like a cancer in nine–year–old Eddie. Inside he gradually became cold and hard. It was the only way he could cope with the daily jibes. Finally Eddie decided to run away, back to his beloved Granda.

It was like being let out of jail! Granda's house was completely different. It was an open house. The kettle was never off and great pots of steaming soup filled the kitchen with a hungry–making aroma.

Eddie never knew what he'd find cluttering up the room when he came home from school—bits of cars or motorbikes, broken chairs or other furniture that needed mending. People were always coming to buy or sell things because Granda was wheeling and dealing in just about everything.

The house was just as busy at night because Granda loved music—Scottish music. He'd take out his old accordion, sit on a kitchen chair at the window and play for hours. There'd be music and drinking and singing and people crowding in to enjoy it all.

Granda always had time for Eddie. He taught him how to use his hands and make things with wood and metal. And he taught him how to fight. 'Come on—let's see what you're made of,' Granda would say. To Granda, being able to handle yourself in a fight was one of life's basic necessities. He saw to it that Eddie learned that lesson well.

School days

By the time Eddie reached Old Aberdeen Secondary School he was known as a 'hard case'. Most lessons meant little or nothing to him, though he didn't mind practical subjects.

The only times Eddie looked forward to at school were the breaks. Then he could go out and do what he most enjoyed—fight. His early rejection made him ultra–sensitive to remarks the other boys made and he often took them the wrong way, deliberately magnifying an innocent comment into a reason to lash out. His own inner hurt fuelled his desire to see others hurt in turn.

If school days were not the happiest days of his life, the nights were much more satisfactory to Eddie. He was free to roam around as he liked as long as he was in before eleven. Granda would sit and wait until his son Michael came in and once he was in, Granda would lock the door and go off to his bed, his household safely locked up for the night.

17

Or so he thought. For that was the time when Eddie would be ready for going out again. This time it was through the window and down the drainpipe. He'd meet up with lads older than himself and roam the streets until two or three o'clock, returning via the drainpipe.

Their main hang-out was a city-centre graveyard. It was the era of the skinheads. Both boys and girls had their own gear. Eddie and the others would sit around, looking out for guys with motorbikes. Some nights they'd go really wild after a few drinks and their gangs would tear up Union Street, fling a hammer through a shop window and grab what they wanted—a bottle of wine, jewellery, whatever. The place would suddenly be full of bobbies, but that all added to the sport. There was little the police could do in all the confusion of the gangs. Such excitement was the breath of life to the young teenager.

One night there was a big fight between some school kids—the Powis boys and the Froghall lads. Although he was their age, Eddie had been trained in a much tougher school. The kids had never seen anybody fight like him before.

In the midst of the action Eddie picked up

a big stone and threw it. Then he heard folk screaming that one of the boys had been hit in the head. To Eddie it was all in the game. If they couldn't cope with that kind of fighting, they shouldn't be there. It could happen to anybody; it was one of the risks. You had to take your chance.

Rossie Farm

Eddie was sure that he could get away with his misdeeds. 'I'm only fourteen,' he thought confidently. 'They can't touch me.' But the members of the Children's Panel thought otherwise. He was put on remand to Rossie Farm, Montrose.

'Looks like a school,' he thought as they turned in at the gates. 'I wonder what kinda place it is?'

He soon found out. Ordinary lessons did go on, but there was also gardening, bricklaying, cooking, dining-hall work and laundry. There was even some farm work with potatoes and carrots. After teatime came recreation—TV, darts, snooker, and pool. But none of these really interested Eddie. All he thought about was how he could get away.

Soon afterwards Eddie found himself assigned to the 'garden party'. He was shown how to use a petrol lawnmower and told to cut the grass. 'Fine,' thought Eddie. 'Here's my chance!'

For a while he tramped up and down the grass after the lawnmower. Then, when he was sure no–one was around, he tied the pull–cord by its flex to a tree, its motor still making a nice even purr, while he slipped away through on to the railway line and headed off in the direction of Arbroath, the next town further south.

His freedom didn't last long and when the authorities caught up with him they hauled him back to Rossie Farm. For his next escape Eddie collaborated with three other lads but it wasn't long before the cops gave chase and they were all caught.

It might have been quite a lark when you were out, but it certainly wasn't much fun when you got back! Eddie found out the hard way that there were two little cells in Rossie Farm which the Headmaster used to administer a punishment known as jump-ups—sharp strokes of a belt laid across bare buttocks! You might be awarded four or five, but sometimes as many as a dozen!

One day Eddie broke out again, and this time he stayed out for several months.

He had a high old time, breaking and entering to steal money, clothes, drink, anything he fancied. He slept rough most of the time, but he kept himself smart by using the public toilets for a wash and shave.

Travelling by night, he moved about between Montrose, Arbroath and Aberdeen and then hitched a lift to Banff where his mother and Granda were now living quite close to each other. He had no intention of going in to Granda's house, but he knew that there was an old wooden garage behind the house with an old Austin Seven car inside. It would be a good place to sleep.

For a day or two he managed to feed himself by stealing food from the neighbouring houses when the folk were out. But then his Mum spotted him. Inevitably, Granda caught sight of her crossing the yard one day with a plate of chips half–hidden under her coat.

'Eddie's in the shed,' he challenged when she came back.

'No, he's nae,' she denied. But Granda knew better.

'You'd better get him in the hoose. He's nae stayin' ootside,' the old man insisted. So Eddie moved up into the loft and stayed with them for some time. Then one night they had a lot of visitors and somebody went to the police and told them where Eddie was.

He spent the night in the police station and next morning a car came to drive him back to Rossie Farm. As they were passing through Aberdeen the car stopped at a red light. Quick as a flash Eddie nipped out, jumped over a fence and into the grounds of a hospital. He was away again, but not for long.

What were the authorities to do with him? Although he was only fourteen it was decided to admit him to Aberdeen's adult prison, Craiginches, until various reports could be obtained from social and psychiatric workers.

Craiginches

So it was that Eddie found himself in Craiginches. 'To pot with it!' he told himself. 'I'm here. I must be as bad as they are. I'll show 'em!'

The door opened to admit a man with big scars on his face. 'You all right, wee man?' he asked.

Eddie reacted in instant fury. 'Who're you

calling wee man? I'm nae little! Get shot! I'm no' a mug.'

The man shrugged. 'Follow me,' he ordered. 'They've put you in B Hall.' Eddie followed the man through a door and suddenly found himself in a huge hall with long corridors of doors. Everything was strangely quiet. The men were all walking about like zombies. Many of them had slash scars on their faces. He was taken to a cell and the door locked behind him. This was it! He was in jail–a brickwork cell with a light stuck in the wall, a wee board for posters and a concrete floor. He didn't need to examine the bed to know it was filthy. The stink of urine on the dirty blankets was unmistakable and powerful. The new routine started at 6.00 a.m. next day. Someone opened his door, looked in, checked whether there were one or two inmates, then banged the door shut again. He went the whole length of the corridor … bang, bang, bang!

Thoroughly awakened by the racket, Eddie heard the prison officers shouting, '35 on second, 44 on the top, 30 on the bottom'. If the total numbers proved nobody was missing the next cry was: 'Open 'em up.'

Once the doors were opened Eddie found

you had to take your 'pot' along the corridor, slop it out and wash it. Then you got water in a basin and took it back into your cell to wash yourself. When that had been emptied, you sat in your cell until 7.00 a.m. when it was breakfast time. Immediately after breakfast you were locked up until 11 a.m. when you were taken into a small yard for exercise. Locked up again until lunch and dinner time, and after that locked up again for the night. You were locked up for almost twenty-three hours a day!

For once in his life Eddie had little to do but think—and plenty of time to do it in! Strangely enough he didn't mind too much. He decided that, in spite of the poor quality of food, and never having enough of it, he would do all he could to keep himself fit. So he gradually built up his 'score' of press–ups and in between these he indulged in wildly aggressive fantasies. His aggressive tendencies sometimes got him in real trouble and he was punished in 'solitary'. It satisfied something deep inside Eddie to use his time in solitary positively. Hadn't Granda trained him always to benefit from whatever situation he was in? He certainly wasn't going to let this beat him.

Borstals and breakaways

The next stop was Borstal, at Polmont. There was no high wall round the young offender's institution like Craiginches, but it was a huge building and all the windows were barred. The cells here were polished and everything else was the same—all spick and span and clean. The prison officers didn't wear uniforms but suits.

Eddie wondered what other differences he would find. What really hit him was the strict regime. Their curt way of giving orders roused instant rebellion in Eddie. 'Get your hair cut!'

'You're nae gonna cut my hair!' Eddie protested.

But they banged him down and cut his hair really short.

'Now get a shave!'

'I dinna shave.' But he had to, even though his beard had barely started to grow.

It all added up to an atmosphere of intense pressure.

In Borstal, tension seemed to be in the air they breathed and fights among the men often broke out. Eddie and another guy were fighting one day, but they stopped when they saw an officer approaching. They agreed to carry on later.

They had decided to fight in the toilet block where they would be more or less out of sight. They had just started going for each other, and were getting really stuck in, their heavy blows making blood flow freely, when a prison officer appeared. Immediately both men ran, Eddie back to the dormitory. He tore off his blood-stained shirt, grabbed someone else's and by the time the prison officer arrived he was sitting on his bed.

'On your feet!' Everybody in the dormitory sprang to attention beside their beds, Eddie included. The officer paced the room, and reaching Eddie, hit him an almighty swipe on his face. Eddie fell back across his bed. Anger coursed through his body, but his mind flashed a warning. 'Keep it … keep it. This is no' the time. They're just wanting you in the cells to interrogate you. Keep quiet.'

The officer stood over Eddie. 'You slashed a guy … you just missed killing him. You got him in the throat,' he accused.

'I dinna ken nothing aboot it,' Eddie insisted.

Eddie felt pretty scared. Had he really hurt the guy as badly as the officer said? 'What am

I going to do with this one?' he wondered. 'I could get five years for this. How am I going to get out of it?'

An idea came to Eddie. 'I'm gonna cut my wrist. As soon as I cut it, you hit that bell. Get the screws in. You've got to do this for me 'cos if they can fix this on me I'm gonna face four or five years', he told the eleven lads sharing the dormitory.

He glanced round the group, willing them to agree.

'OK, Eddie.'

He sliced his wrist. Blood flowed. The guys hit the bell. The door opened and officers rushed in, grabbed Eddie and took him straight down to the doctor. Once he was stitched up he was taken to 'solitary'. A single tiny light shone in the darkness of the cell and Eddie was ordered to sit on the one hard chair until told to move to his bed for the night.

It was a crazy stint but he got away with it.

But with the end of his sentence freedom came at last. And Eddie knew what he had to do, for he had received news from his mother. Bad news. Granda was ill. Very ill. He had to go and see him before it was too late.

2. Angry young man

'What do I have to show for my life?'

'Yer Granda's nae weel. An' he's hopin' tae see ye soon.'

Eddie stuffed his mother's letter back into his pocket as the train carried him north to Aberdeen and then on to Banff, and Granda.

It was a shock to see the old man looking so frail. He had always been so strong, so full of life. But Granda was pleased to see Eddie. Pleased, but realistic.

'I've only lasted this long 'cos I wanted to see ye again,' he murmured when the stocky teenager stood beside his bed.

A few days later Granda died. Nobody was surprised. But his death hit Eddie like a body blow. He stumbled blindly outside into the yard and across to the shed. Recent rain had made the place into a morass of mud. Eddie flung himself headlong into it. What did it matter that he was wearing a completely new outfit provided by his uncle? Suit, shirt, tie, sweater—all became filthy with mud as Eddie rolled around, as deep, angry sobs were wrenched from his body.

The future lay blank before him. What was he going to do now? At sixteen what schooling he'd had was over. So he accepted his mother's offer and agreed to stay on in Banff for a while. He might even get a job.

In that, he was fortunate. Painter and decorator Bill Anderson offered to take him on as an apprentice. 'I'll give you a chance because you've told me the truth about being in prison. I know you've had problems.'

Eddie realised he had been lucky to be taken on at all at sixteen. Apprentices usually started at fifteen. So he stuck it for a while. But he was used to having far more money at his disposal. His weekly wages seemed a mere pittance by comparison. So he gradually started supplementing them in the old way, taking what he fancied. Especially cars.

Of course, in time, he got caught. He found

himself up on several charges: theft, driving without insurance, road tax or MOT. He was awarded nine months for each offence, to run concurrently, and was sent to a Young Offenders prison at Friarton, Perth. He was not slow to make the most of the 'education' offered. In Perth he learned how to 'do' alarm systems, quietly putting them out of action. He discovered how to rip the backs off safes and how to use plastic explosives safely. 'Some of these guys are really talented and gifted at getting into places,' he confided to a newcomer. 'You can learn a lot here.'

Eddie's unruliness earned him a transfer to Perth. Here not all of his activity was negative. He did quite a lot of keep-fit training—press-ups and weight training. It was equally important to keep yourself 'psyched up' mentally. When your cell door opened you never knew whether there might be a guy coming flying in with a knife or intent on some other kind of hassle. You needed eyes in the back of your head when you walked about the jail. You really needed to know what was going on.

But jail sentences always came to an end sooner or later, as one did when Eddie was nineteen. He made his way to Aberdeen and went into a pub called East Neuk. He knew this was a really tough pub. Walking up to the bar he placed his order.

'A pint of wa'er and fill it wi' salt.'

'What?' The barmaid stared at him in disbelief. Eddie repeated his order, adding: 'I've got a sair stomach. I dinna ken what it is, maybe an ulcer. I've heard that's good for it.'

It was a load of rubbish, but he liked the look of the lassie and at least now he had her interest. As they chatted on he discovered that her brother owned the pub. It wasn't long before he was going steady with Marion and was taken on to work as a 'bouncer' in the pub. The job proved harder and rougher than he'd imagined, sorting out fights or physically removing men who were dead drunk—and heavy.

Marion was under no illusions about the kind of man Eddie was as their courtship continued, especially as he moved into her flat before they got married. But they were strongly attracted to each other so that, when Eddie was facing a court case in Banff she went with him to the hearing. On the bus she tried to reassure him. 'I'll write to you when you're in jail, Eddie. I'll wait for you. However long it is.'

But Eddie refused to be reassured. 'This is rubbish,' he thought. 'I know what'll happen once I'm in there. She'll send me a "Dear John," even though she is expecting.'

Later they sat close together in the courtroom, silently waiting for the hammer. The judge looked them both up and down before pronouncing sentence. He made a few general comments on the case and then concluded: 'This time I believe you are genuinely sorry for what you have done. Because you intend to get married and your girlfriend is expecting I will give you a two year sentence—deferred.'

For the first time in his life Eddie said 'Thank you' to a judge, and meant it. It was the first time a judge had been willing to give him another chance. He determined not to waste it.

He did make an honest attempt to settle down, especially when his son, Peter James, was born. He managed to find first one job and then another, but the sort of work he got never paid the kind of money Eddie felt he needed. It was just too easy to supplement it in the way he knew best—stealing it from other people.

After a while Eddie decided to become officially self–employed. Unknown to Marion he borrowed money from her brother and other friends, bought himself a big black van, and became a slater. But that was only part of the story. As he was working on the roof slates he'd look through the windows to see what was available. Then he would make a return visit at night and remove jewellery, videos or whatever he fancied.

When another baby was on the way they moved to another house in Stewart Park, but Eddie's behaviour didn't change. Marion became suspicious and, when he came home very late one night, she was waiting.

'Where have you been?' she demanded. And then, when Eddie refused to answer, 'You were out with somebody else.'

'No, I wasna', Eddie lied. She couldn't prove it, so why worry? But he knew his marriage was in tatters. Marion was doing all she could, but he just couldn't cope with being married and tied down. It was too much. He moved out and went back to his mother, who now lived in Aberdeen's Grandholm Estate.

Shortly afterwards Eddie's second son, Stewart, was born. He saw the baby only twice. Then Marion made the break.

'Wi' all your carryin' on and your hassle, I canna cope. I don't want to know you.'

That was it. The marriage was finished.

Twenty-one marked Eddie's entry into an adult prison, and the 'key of the door' turned behind him in Craiginches, Aberdeen, after yet another offence.

At first Eddie found it a scary situation—the whole routine was different.

You got up at 6 a.m., had breakfast and went straight to work until the 12 o'clock lunch. From 1 to 2 p.m. you had exercise and then worked again until 4 o'clock teatime. At 4.30 p.m. you were locked up for the night. Only after three months were you allowed evening recreation such as TV or snooker. So Eddie found he had hours to spend sitting on a chair, thinking.

'What a waste it all is! Here I am back in prison and what have I to show for my life?' he mused despondently. 'My marriage is finished, and even though I have two sons, I might never see them again.' The feeling of hurt and loss bit deep now that he had time to think about it. Why was it that he seemed to destroy everything he put his hand on? Why did he always lose the people he loved – or just throw them away?

However long he thought about it, he couldn't work out the reason. He only knew that his whole situation depressed him. But what could he do?

Then one day a tiny incident triggered an unexpectedly violent response.

It happened when a prison officer came in to his cell. Seeing a packet of biscuits on Eddie's table he helped himself to one. Eddie said nothing, but inwardly he was seething with resentment. He almost told the man where to go, but somehow managed to hold his tongue.

When the officer had gone Eddie strode across to the sheds where the men were working. 'What's wrong, Eddie?'

'I'm fed up, that's what!' Eddie spat the words out angrily. 'Look, you guys move away. Something's gonna happen.'

He quickly spotted a couple of men he knew, one serving a life sentence. He'd know how to help.

'I'm wanting to do a bit of damage. What would be the best thing to use?'

'What about that big iron bar?' the man suggested, indicating the head–height metal support used for making Army camouflage nets—one of the regular occupations in the prison.

Eddie checked it. It would suit him fine. When the time came, at two o'clock,when all the men were working, Eddie walked into the long barn-like workshed. In one half men were sitting on stools, using knitting machines. In the other half men were working on the camouflage nets. Rising from shoulder height a series of thick, unbreakable glass windows separated the two working areas. Only three or four of the men knew about his plan and they were surreptitiously watching him, waiting for something to happen. Sitting on a stool, Eddie himself was waiting.

He hadn't quite figured out exactly when he was going to move but he could feel the gut reaction building up inside. His nerves always felt the same whenever he was going to do anything nasty. Part of him was dead scared, but this only helped him to psyche himself up for the moment of action. It came. He flew off his seat, gave the iron bar a hefty kick and, using all his strength, ripped it out of the wall. For a second he stood there, panting, holding the solid metal bar in the air.

Then, before anybody knew what was going on, he started smashing the windows in the glass divider screen. Splintering glass showered in all directions as he worked his way along, swinging the iron bar with such force that the wooden frames were knocked out along with the glass. Prisoners ran as they were ordered outside. Riot bells clamoured and squads of prison officers came flying in. Chaos reigned as Eddie continued to smash his way along the heavy glass windows.

He even took time to shout to the officers: 'Come near me and you're gettin' it!'

Few approached, he noticed. They were intent on getting the place clear before any other prisoners joined in with him.

Then an officer known as Tattie Jim took a few steps towards him. Eddie swung the bar high over his head. He was all ready to lash out and crash his weapon over the man's head. But something made him pull back.

'You're nae worth it,' he muttered, flinging the bar down to the ground. In the nick of time he'd realised what the consequences would be if he killed a prison officer. It just wasn't worth it.

The mind—games, the hassles, the tensions, the fights continued for the rest of his sentence. Sometimes, at the height of his violence, Eddie realised that he was totally confused. It was as if he was somehow inwardly forced to do things that he wouldn't normally do. He would think: 'I dinna want to do that, but I've got to do that.' What was driving him? Eddie just didn't know.

A new romance

Released once more Eddie went to stay with his mum in Aberdeen and discovered a new hobby, Citizen Band radio.

He and his brother Bill stayed up till all hours either speaking or listening, enjoying their contact with complete strangers. One night when Bill was operating the CB a woman's voice answered him. Eddie grabbed the mike.

'Hey, you've got a real sexy voice. What about an eyeball?'

'Now?' the voice queried. 'It's two o'clock in the morning!'

'So what?' said Eddie. 'Tell me where I can pick you up and I'll come flying on the bike.'

Minutes later Eddie roared off to meet the owner of the sexy voice at the roundabout near

39

Dyce airport. It did occur to him on the way that she might not show up—it was a bit of a crazy stunt. But she was there all right and she was not alone; her friend and an aunt were with her. What's more she looked as good as she'd sounded, Eddie decided.

Sally was up from England for a week's holiday, staying with her friend's aunt. Eddie made sure he saw plenty of her during that week and he even went back to London with her for a further week. Their acquaintance deepened so swiftly that he was able to persuade her to return to Aberdeen and live with him at his Auntie Tricia's house.

It wasn't long before Sally became pregnant, so they got married, and went to live in a council flat. Before long Eddie fell into the old routine of heavy drinking and going out with other women, though he kept as much as he could from Sally. A baby daughter, Anna, was born.

If Sally was loyal to him, Eddie did not return the compliment. He drank heavily, went out with other women when it suited him, and acquired most of his money by stealing. He did get caught and charged for some of his thefts, but usually managed to get bail. Not that he let a little thing like bail curb his activities.

Somehow he managed to keep it all from Sally. One night he took her and another couple out for a slap–up meal on the proceeds. The other man was, like himself, out on bail. On the way back to the house the man warned him to expect the police. 'Somebody's grassed us off,' he said.

Once they got home Eddie loaded his stolen car with the stolen goods and went off and sold them to another of his friends. Then he took the number plates off the car, dumped them and set fire to the vehicle.

* * * *

Eddie was charged with theft and threatening and intimidating a witness and sentenced to two and a half years in Saughton prison, Edinburgh. This time he started by behaving well, hoping to get out quicker and perhaps even get parole. Later he was transferred to Dumfries, in the very south of Scotland, where he managed to wangle a job in the bakery. He enjoyed the work and even managed to make a bit of money.

It was in Dumfries that Sally visited him.

With Eddie in prison, she had had time to

think. She was disillusioned with him, hating his lying and drinking. So she decided to go back to live in England to be near her parents. She let their house go and moved south with her baby. Once settled, she came to Dumfries to visit Eddie.

At the time Eddie was on Valium to help control his fighting tendencies. The drug slurred his speech, and Sally could make no sense of what he said to her. It wasn't long before he started receiving letters which aroused his suspicions.

'Something's no' right,' he muttered, as he read. But the letters continued to arrive, though at growing intervals, and he consoled himself as each one was read to him that at least it wasn't that most dreaded of all letters, a 'Dear John'. Not yet.

In the end the letters stopped arriving. Then, on Christmas Day, he was handed a letter in his cell. It was from Sally. The gist of it was in the final paragraph.

'The last time I saw you, you were stoned out of your mind. It's obvious you don't want to change, so we'll just call it quits.'

The dreaded 'Dear John' had come at last!

3. From darkness to light

A journey into life

Rejection, regret and sheer rage hit Eddie as he stared at the sheet of paper in his hand. He'd half expected it for ages.

'How can I get out on parole if she's no' wantin' me?' he asked himself desperately. 'And what about my daughter? If she's taken her to England, will I ever see her again?'

Black misery settled over Eddie. He then remembered it was Christmas Day. 'But you don't get letters in prison on Christmas Day,' he thought.

Eddie grabbed the letter again and looked at the date. It had been posted several days earlier. Even allowing for the Christmas rush, it must have been lying around in the prison, Eddie decided. He slammed his fist on the table.

'They've done it on purpose,' he raged. 'They kept this "Dear John" until today on purpose. They wanted to hurt me. They're just animals!'

Eddie let rip, shouting and swearing, spewing out his hurt and anger for all to hear. Men in neighbouring cells heard the uproar and began to bang on their doors.

All sorts of mad schemes flashed through his mind as he went to the kitchen. Should he cook up a solution of boiling water laced heavily with sugar and throw it in the officers' faces? No. He'd do something worse than that … something which would be worth being punished for!

He decided on a different plan. He went back up to his cell and just shut up. Instead of arguing and swearing, he stayed dead quiet. When anyone came and asked him if he was all right, he didn't reply. Different people came and spoke pleasantly to him, willing to listen and try to help, but they all got the same response. Silence.

The Governor prescribed three days in the punishment cells, after which he was judged fit to return to work in the kitchen. But his mind continued to focus on what harm he could do. There was one prison officer he hated particularly, a man who had a weakness for drink and kept a store of it hidden away.

The officer he had his eye on worked with him in the kitchen as a cook, so Eddie started to keep a watch on his movements. The man soon sensed his hostility and became very nervy. Eddie's pals also knew what was going on in his mind and when they saw him standing with one of the long, steel kitchen knives in his hand, they would persuade him to hand it over.

'Away up the stairs, Eddie,' they'd advise. It was behaviour like this which sometimes resulted in Eddie being put back in a cell for a night to quieten him down. Unfortunately it did not always have this effect.

Tension never left him in those days. The smallest thing could cause him to flare up. One day an inmate passed by and spoke with an English accent. That was enough for Eddie. Wasn't his wife English? Look what she'd done to him! Without warning he jumped out and grabbed the guy, threw him into a cell and started kicking him and punching him in the face.

* * * *

'Have you anything to say?'

'Nothing to say.' It was his favourite response.

As a result he spent most of the next forty days in solitary confinement. This suited Eddie. Maybe he could sort out his thoughts now.

He could not have guessed how an unexpected visitor would revolutionise his plans.

Eddie was in his cell and had just started eating his evening meal of mince, tatties, and bread, with a big mug of tea to follow, when a visitor arrived. It was a Church of Scotland minister, the Rev. Bill McKenzie. He came in, greeted Eddie and said he had come to talk about Jesus.

'But I want to ha'e my grub,' Eddie thought, eyeing the stranger.

But he said nothing. There was something about the guy that made him feel he might be worth listening to.

'You want to eat your dinner?' McKenzie asked.

'It's all right.' Eddie suddenly found his dinner could wait after all. He was more hungry for conversation than for food, and there was something about this guy which appealed to Eddie.

So the meal slowly went cold as the two men sat and talked together.

'Jesus really wants to come into your life …' McKenzie began.

'But look at me!' Eddie interrupted. Might as well let him have it straight. 'My life's in a mess, pal. I've naethin'.'

As he listened to what McKenzie said about Jesus, Eddie found he couldn't feel sorry for himself any more. But he didn't want the guy to go on speaking about Jesus. He wanted to speak about himself!

Suddenly Eddie found he was pouring out the sorry story of his life and wrecked marriage. McKenzie listened to it all and then offered to write to Sally to see if things could be sorted out.

But Eddie was adamant. 'Just leave it,' he said. 'It would be a waste of time. She's made her decision. Just leave it.'

'Okay. If that's what you want,' McKenzie said, rising to his feet. 'But I'll be back.' Before he left he handed Eddie a booklet. 'I'll leave this with you to read,' he said as the officer came to open the door.

Eddie looked at the booklet, *Journey Into Life*.

'If God really was alive like you said,' he thought, 'he'd have told you I dinna ken how to read, pal. What a joke!'

Eddie began to feel annoyed that he had shared more with him than he had ever done with anyone in his life before. Why had he done it? A renewed sense of anger incited him to put everything he'd got into the press–ups. He was really psyching himself up now. He started running on the spot, expending all his energy.

Then he rang the bell and asked to go to the toilet. Four prison officers escorted him as usual. On the way back Eddie spotted a heap of books lying on a table so he grabbed one, slipped it inside his shirt and went back to the cell.

Once inside he spelt out the title: *Hooked*. At that stage his reading was at the 'c–a–t, d–o–g' stage. Longer words were a mystery to him. Somehow he picked up that book and read it from cover to cover. It took all night, yet he read without stopping and managed to finish the whole book. It was something he had never done before in his life.

'I've got a book here,' he shouted to the guy in the next cell. 'Would you like to read it?'

'What's it called?'

'*Hooked,*' Eddie replied, hoping he was right.

'I've read it,' the guy said.

'What's the story about then?' Eddie asked, eager to check if he really had managed to read, but without letting the other guy know he couldn't. As the man went through the story Eddie realised it was exactly what he'd read. So he hadn't imagined it. He really had read a book!

Immediately he went and picked up the discarded *Journey Into Life* booklet and read it from cover to cover. On the last page he found an invitation to ask Jesus into his life. Without hesitation Eddie asked Jesus not once, but six times to come into his life and take over. He didn't know what he was expected to feel – if anything. But he actually felt nothing at all. No difference. So had anything happened?

Towards the end of his time in solitary the Governor came to Eddie's cell and said, 'I've been hearing good things about you, Murison. I think we'll put you back into circulation. Somehow I don't feel as if there's going to be any more hassle.'

Eddie felt suddenly confused. What was

happening? He gathered his personal belongings into a bundle to go back upstairs, but his head began to throb. He realised he really didn't want to go back to normal prison life with all the noise of banging doors and rattling keys. He'd grown to enjoy the quietness down here where he was free to think his own thoughts. Especially these last weeks.

Next morning, after the normal breakfast time, he padded barefoot down to the canteen, clad only in pyjama bottoms, all of which was against the rules.

'Where's my breakfast?' he asked.

His old enemy, the cook, came right up to him. 'There's something different about you, Eddie. Your eyes aren't black any more.' Eddie knew he meant the hatred had gone from them. 'I'm not scared of you any more. I feel at peace with you.'

Now Eddie was the one who was scared! 'I must be getting soft,' he thought as he carried his breakfast back to his cell, totally confused. 'What's goin' on here?' he asked himself. 'That guy should be scared o' me. What's the problem? Something's happening. I'm gettin' soft.'

It was a few minutes before he realised: 'I asked Jesus into my life. So he is in. It must be him who has taken away the bitterness and anger and is making me soft.'

Then fear struck—it was no good being soft in prison. You never knew who would try to plunge you. He'd have to put up a front again … pretend to be tough, like he was before. Inside, though, he knew he was a different guy.

Before long he was living a different life quite openly. He started attending Bible studies and even getting men into his cell to read the Bible with him. They used the Gideon Bibles which were around in the prison. Maybe a few were nicked from the Chapel, but at least they were being read and studied. They prayed together as well, asking God to help them to get to know him better, to keep them safe and help them to talk about Jesus to any of the men who would listen. Not surprisingly they became known as the God Squad.

All this happened at a time when many prisons were experiencing sudden outbreaks of violence, and it was rumoured that some of the inmates of Dumfries were to be transferred to a new prison at Shotts to make room for some of the troublemakers. Eddie rather fancied a look at Shotts.

But it was not to be. Of the ten men who were Christians, nine were moved to Shotts. Eddie was sent north to Glenochil. Under the same rearrangement scheme many of the hardest cases from Peterhead prison were being transferred to Glenochil, while men who were considered to need protection were being sent to Peterhead.

Release

The thought that he might lose his faith really scared Eddie. He felt he'd only just found Jesus and he meant so much to him. But what would happen in a strange prison on his own?

On his first day at Glenochil a man approached and started to make conversation. He was a quiet–looking, bearded man and Eddie was instantly wary. He decided to speak out boldly.

'Where's the Bible classes here?' he asked. He'd decided that making a stand at the start might help him hang on to his faith.

'You a Christian as well?' the man enquired.

'Are you?' Eddie countered, determined not to be the first to give anything away. Even when the man admitted he was, Eddie asked him a few salient questions just to be sure!

As they chatted, Eddie discovered that the man had been a police officer but he was serving six years for armed robbery. Which made him a prime target for the other inmates, Eddie realised. 'Maybe God has put me here to keep him safe,' he thought. 'Maybe I'm here to see that nobody damages him.'

At Glenochil Eddie had started to attend the meetings held by members of the Prison Fellowship and Eddie Macguire, one of the PF visitors, asked,' How long have you got left to serve, Eddie?'

'Six weeks.'

'How'd you like to come and stay with my family for a while when you get out?' Macguire offered.

Eddie went to the Governor and asked if he could get out for a weekend to go and stay with a Christian family to see if he thought he could fit in there.

'Be sensible, Murison. You're doing time. You're not getting out.'

It was no use arguing so Eddie phoned Macguire to let him know the outcome. Macguire understood. But then Eddie spoke to God. 'I'm nae acceptin' this, Lord,' he said. 'I'm wantin' oot to see if I'm gonna fit into this or no'. He requested another interview.

This time it was the Deputy Governor who saw him. He made his request as before.

'Yes,' came the reply. 'I don't see why not.'

'You'll get out on Sunday at ten o'clock in the morning. You're to be back by twenty past four.'

When he knew he was going to be allowed out, Eddie began to get ideas. If he could get hold of some drugs while he was 'outside' and smuggle them back in, he could make a tidy bit of money which could be very useful when he was released. But even as he made his arrangements, Eddie was conscious that he wasn't just planning to do wrong. He was intending to commit a deliberate sin. The thought made him unexpectedly uncomfortable – guilty – as if he had a heavy burden right on top of his head.

'I've got to tell you,' Eddie admitted to Maguire. 'I'm here – oot – and I'm planning to take drugs back in. But I can't do it. I'm a Christian. I can't do that any more.'

Macguire nodded understandingly. 'Don't worry about it. It needn't go any further. If you really believe in God, he'll look after you. Just leave it at that.'

All too soon it was time to go back to prison and face the guys who were expecting the drugs he hadn't brought back. He knew it wouldn't be easy. Could God really protect him? He remembered a fellow Christian from another Hall. At exercise time Eddie ran over to him.

'You've got to pray for me—my life's in danger here,' he said, and explained about the drug episode.

'If it's gonna happen, you've just got to stand for it, Eddie,' the man said.

'I canna hit back I know, but ...'

'Tell them Jesus loves you,' his friend suggested.

'I don't know if I can do that, man,' Eddie admitted. 'I don't think I'm there. I don't think I've that kind of faith.'

His paranoia made him barricade his door at night, yet still he didn't feel safe. He even told a prison officer that his life was in danger.

Locked in his cell that night Eddie appealed to God. 'Lord, I need you,' was all he said. But as he spoke the words, Eddie felt himself suddenly filled with peace, a total and complete peace, such as he had never experienced before. Next morning his door was opened at ten o'clock and the prison staff just disappeared. Eddie felt they guessed there was going to be a big fight and they just walked away.

But Eddie knew just what he was going to do. He went straight to the guy who intended to knife him, put his hand in and pulled the knife out of the man's waistband.

'Jesus doesna' want that,' he said. 'Jesus loves you.'

Eddie threw the knife down, and he could feel love rising up inside him for the guy—not his own love but the love of Jesus, flowing out. It was a strange, new feeling. It made him want to tell the other guy, and his mates, about what Jesus had for them.

A short time later the four men were sitting in Eddie's cell. He sat there totally alert, his back straight, head down over his toes, poised for action. At the least movement he was going right in – head first. He would pulp the guy who made the wrong move. There was no way he was going to allow himself to be stabbed with only a week to go. But even as he sat there he could feel the love of God inside him. He began preaching to the men, sharing with them all the things he had learnt in Dumfries prison. Somehow the words were just spilling out of his lips.

'I'm a Christian. I believe in Jesus,' he told them. 'I don't want to go back into this kind of rubbish. I'm finished with this kinda life. And God can do the same for you if you open up and just listen to what I'm saying. Jesus loves you. He can help you. Crime's no' right—'

Suddenly one of the guys interrupted him. 'Part o' me wants to walk out of the door, but the other part o' me wants to stay here.'

'Praise the Lord, man!' Eddie shouted. 'That shows that Jesus is here.'

An almost tangible peace filled the cell. All the fears, paranoia and aggression had gone right out of the window.

The last few days passed uneventfully and suddenly the morning of his release from prison arrived. He was sitting in the 'dub box', the tiny room where prisoners changed their clothes. All at once he was overcome by a rush of doubts.

'Is it right to go to Macguire's house?' he asked himself. 'Maybe I should go back to Aberdeen, hit the bevvie, get a woman and have a right carry on? Get some money...' The old way of life leered at him, with its own insidious invitation.

Part Two:
Training for Freedom

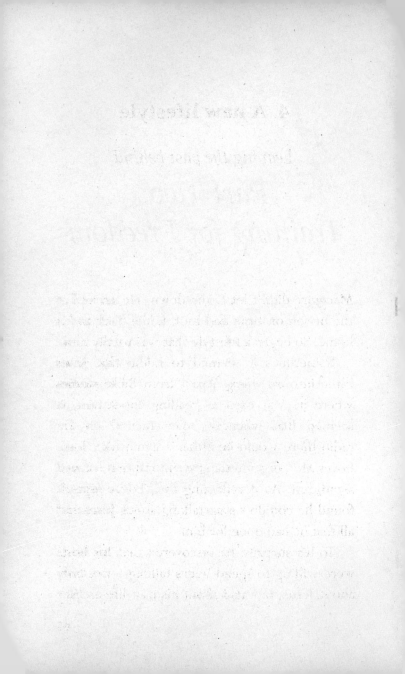

4. A new lifestyle

'Leaving the past behind'

Macguire didn't let Eddie down. He arrived at the prison on time and took Eddie back to his home. So began a lifestyle that was totally new.

Sometimes it seemed to Eddie that Jesus came into *everything*. Apart from Bible studies where he was used to reading about him, it seemed that whenever they turned on the radio there would be either a hymn like 'Jesus Loves Me', or something scriptural that seemed significant. As if reflecting this, Eddie himself found he couldn't stop talking about Jesus and all that he had done for him.

To his surprise he discovered that his hosts were willing to spend hours talking—not only about Jesus, but also about his past life as they tried to help him sort things out.

It took just two and a half weeks before crisis hit Eddie. He woke up one day and knew that he was totally confused. He was enjoying his new life and in one way he felt good, but in another he felt as if he no longer knew who he really was. He knew that God was changing him, filling him, washing him clean from what he'd been. But he also felt that God was asking him to give himself 100 per cent to him. That thought threw Eddie into confusion.

'I can't do it, God,' he groaned. 'I couldna give you a 100 per cent, I don't know how. I'm nae good enough.'

The spiritual change had been real all right, but he felt he just couldn't continue. That was when he told the Macguires, 'I've got to go away tomorrow.' 'I've been thinking about some money I stole,' he said. 'I want to give it back. I'll go and give it to the police in Aberdeen. I'll come back doon here after,' he promised.

It was a downright lie. The thoughts in his head were quite different.

Eddie packed his few belongings together and next morning took the train to Aberdeen. But Eddie soon found that God was not as

62

easy to run away from as Macguire had been. Walking along Aberdeen's main thoroughfare, Union Street, a few days later he happened to glance up a side street. The words *Abbey Christian Fellowship* caught his eye and somehow his feet followed. As if acting under remote control he entered the building and asked to speak to the pastor or whoever was in charge.

While waiting he wandered into the kitchen where two young women were making sandwiches. They offered him a cup of tea, and some of the sandwiches to go with them. As he happily accepted these a tall, well–built man walked in.

'I'm Douglas MacIntyre,' the man said. 'Did you want to see me?'

'I'm a Christian,' Eddie began, 'and I'm nae long out of prison. I've kinda run away from God. But now I'm staying up here and I'm looking for a church.'

'Fine,' said MacIntyre. 'Let's pray.'

So Eddie was back in a church, though he did not settle there easily. He was too mixed up for all that. He still carried a load of guilt about his past life and just couldn't convince himself that he was good enough to be a Christian. On the other hand he resented some of the people who came to church—those who seemed to Eddie to have lots of money, live in big houses and have no problems. He knew he wanted to be in church and to worship God, but he didn't feel he could trust anyone there, or open up to them. So how was he ever going to build up any relationships? Would he ever fit in there?

Then one Sunday morning Douglas MacIntyre preached from Acts, chapter twelve, where an angel touched the imprisoned Peter's side, his chains fell off and he was free. Eddie closed his eyes, thinking that Jesus had done exactly that for *him*, and set *him* free. He felt the tears starting in his eyes.

'Is it all right if I share?' Eddie asked, tears streaming down his face and falling on his pullover.

'Come on up,' MacIntyre invited.

Eddie walked on to the platform and stood in front of the whole church, feeling no fear, just an overwhelming love.

'I've got love inside me,' he began. 'I just want to tell you that I love each and every one of you. I *love* you. and it's Jesus' love … it's nae my love.'

He came off the stage still weeping. From all over the church people spontaneously left their seats and clustered round Eddie. They shook his hand, grabbed his shoulder, even hugged him, mingling their tears of joy with his.

Why then did Eddie hit the bottle at that stage? What made him start drinking whisky and go back to his old way of life? Why did he turn his back on the church – and on God – for the next few months? He stopped living at his mother's house and moved into a mobile home. Even though men from the church visited him there to say they were missing him from the fellowship, it didn't change things. He had been seeing a Christian girl, but now he decided to finish with her too. Once again his life was going rapidly downhill.

One night he and his brother were in a pub when a hefty, bouncer type of man started making advances to his brother's girlfriend.

Eddie had no intention of fighting in front of witnesses. The two men hustled down the stairs and round the back of the pub. To his disgust the man took off his jacket and Eddie tore into him in the old style. He must have hit him about four times before he went down on the deck.

Eddie then started kicking him. He was about to leave him when he saw a big aluminium barrel. He lifted it up above his head and then threw it with all his weight. The missile hit its mark and the man gave a loud grunting sound.

'To pot wi' you,' the unrepentant Eddie said as he picked up the guy's discarded jacket and threw it on a nearby roof. No need to leave evidence lying around.

He went back home. But this was not like the old days. The memory of what he had just done began to exert a fierce and unrelenting pressure. He was totally disgusted with himself.

In the end he went down on his knees. 'Jesus,' he prayed, 'I really repent and ask for forgiveness.'

In the drink sodden recesses of his brain, Eddie knew he had to get help. He had to find somebody who would listen, who would understand about the state he was in.

Two o'clock in the morning found him staggering up to the door of a manse. Swaying unsteadily, Eddie made his plea. 'I need help,' he muttered. 'I've got a drink problem.'

'Right. Come back in the morning and I'll see you,' said the minister.

'You'll see me now,' Eddie insisted. 'If you've got the love of God in you, you'll see me right now!'

Reaching out

The minister eventually managed to persuade Eddie to go home and promised to come and see him next day. He was as good as his word.

I've phoned a place in Fyvie,' the minister said. 'It's a centre for alcoholics and they're willing to take you in. Pack your gear.'

Eddie obeyed, wondering what sort of a place he'd be going to now. Sunnybrae Centre was set in the midst of attractive countryside near Fyvie in Aberdeenshire. The first few days were full of a variety of activities. Counselling sessions and Bible studies were interspersed with weightlifting and games of pool. The first Saturday after he arrived Eddie was encouraged to go to a conference on evangelism and whilst there he made a promise.

'Lord, I need help with drink, but I'm nae gonna work for it. I canna. I made a commitment in jail in front of people, but you'll have to do this for me. If you do, I'll never walk away from you again.'

He returned to Fyvie that afternoon with a renewed interest in Christian things. Once in his room, he took out his Bible. It seemed to fall open at the fifty–first chapter of Isaiah and the words of verse twenty–two leapt out at him.

'This is what your Sovereign Lord says, your God, who defends his people: "See, I have taken out of your hand the cup that made you stagger; from that cup … you will never drink again."' '

The Word came to him with such power that Eddie knew that Jesus had answered the prayer he had prayed at Fyvie! It was an amazing feeling. He praised the Lord for it. Just an hour or two later friends called to see him.

'I'm coming hame wi' you,' Eddie declared. 'I feel fine. God's dealt wi' me.'

Norman, who was in charge of the centre, tried to dissuade him. 'You've only been here a few days, Eddie. Don't run away.'

'But I'm okay,' Eddie insisted. 'Jesus has healed me of drink. I want to go back home.'

Not without some misgivings on the part of the staff, Eddie was, in fact, allowed to leave the Centre with his visitors. No–one could have known then that the word Eddie had received from Isaiah would prove to be a truly prophetic word.

The freedom from dependence on alcohol had an unexpected effect on Eddie. He began to feel a deep concern for alcoholics and the people who lived on the streets of Aberdeen. It was as if something was growing inside him, something he would never have thought possible—a love for hurting people and a determination that something should be done to help them.

The urge to *do* something became stronger and Eddie turned expectantly to his Bible. In Isaiah he found words which seemed like a direct command from the Lord. 'Say to the captives, "Come out," and to those in darkness, "Be free!" They will feed beside the roads and find pasture on every barren hill. They will neither hunger nor thirst. ... He who has compassion on them will guide them and lead them beside springs of water' (Isa. 49: 9-10).

As he read the words over and over again, meditating on them, Eddie knew deep inside him that God wanted him to go and feed the people who were living on the streets, and to preach His Word to them.

He started small by making a few flasks of soup and trekking round the streets where he knew people dossed down for the night. He found them in bushes, boxes, doorways or stretched out on the back seats of buses which were parked for the night. Others were in derelict houses, on benches in Stewart Park or just sleeping out on the beach.

Eddie would gently shake a sleeping figure and say: 'Jesus loves you. Would you like some hot soup?' Then as the man supped the warming liquid, Eddie would encourage him to talk and share his problems. 'Let's pray about this,' Eddie would say, before moving on to search out the next needy person.

Quite soon Eddie was an accepted and most welcome visitor, especially when he started bringing blankets along with the soup. He got some of these from his mother and some from the Salvation Army. In fact, once word got around, it was surprising how people chipped in to help, although much of his own 'dole' money still went on soup. People donated Bibles, and Thermos flasks arrived from as far away as Perth. Whatever the need, God seemed to provide through his people.

Around eight o'clock one morning Eddie was tramping home with his big bags of empty flasks when he met the pastor and an elder of the church. They could not have failed to realise what Eddie had been doing. Shortly after this encounter he was given permission to use the Abbey Fellowship's kitchen premises to cook his soup.

Unexpectedly, a co–worker materialised. Don Robertson, ex–con and drug offender, came to Aberdeen from England, feeling it was where the Lord wanted him to be. Like Eddie, he had been saved while serving a prison sentence, so he understood the problems the street folk were facing and he offered his help. After Eddie and he prayed about it, they started working together.

From these small beginnings a scheme called OFTAN developed. 'Outreach For The Aberdeen Needy' was based in the Abbey Fellowship premises.

Through OFTAN, Eddie didn't aim just to meet people's material needs. He wanted to offer them the Bread of Life, and the Living Water—Jesus. So as people sat informally round the tables after a meal, Eddie or Don would talk to them simply about God and share his word with them. At times someone would bring a guitar and sing songs which also told the Good

News about Jesus and his love for outcasts and strangers.

Romance

Eddie was learning to behave differently too. No longer did he barge through life, intent only on what he wanted. Instead he tried to consider the other person's point of view. He was even losing his fear of people from a different social background, and learning how to handle all his relationships better. Which was just as well, for an important new relationship was right around the corner!

One day, as he was leaving the YMCA, a young woman was walking in. Eddie's response was automatic, and favourable. 'She's nae a bad bit o' stuff,' he thought approvingly, and then went on his way to hand out soup.

He returned to the YMCA the next night. And the next. He discovered that the girl's name was Leslie. When she asked if he would give his testimony again to more of the lads, he agreed.

'I'd like to hear it myself,' Leslie said. Eddie was encouraged. Further acquaintance had confirmed his first opinion and he was definitely interested in pursuing this relationship. Eddie eventually started helping with some of the YM clubs on a regular basis, playing football with the lads, giving short talks, or just sitting chatting, trying to get the kids to open up a bit about their problems. He soon learned that they had real problems, for some of them came from very unhelpful home backgrounds.

One night Leslie offered Eddie a lift home in her car. On the way they called in at her flat for a coffee. Then they decided to have a time of prayer together. Sitting one on each side of the coffee table, they began to pray.

Without any warning a thought came to Eddie as he sat there with closed eyes. 'Look to your right and see your wife.' He dismissed the thought as crazy at once. Leslie was the only other person there and she was sitting opposite him. There was no-one on his right. But when Leslie started to pray he realised that she had moved to kneel beside him on the floor, on his right! Unnerved, he got to his feet and moved away. Leslie opened her eyes, wondering what was happening. She too moved away. They stared at each other across the space.

Eddie's thoughts were running riot. 'What's happenin'? I'm no' interested. I'm wantin'

Jesus. I'm nae wantin' a woman. I've just come through a divorce—the papers'll be here any day. Why all this?' Tense and shaking at the same time, he wondered how he was going to explain himself to the bewildered Leslie.

'What is it?' she asked, unsure of what might happen next. Eddie felt he had to tell her. 'I feel God's saying that you're going to be my wife.' Maybe it sounded stupid, but it was the truth. 'Well He'll have to tell me!' Leslie retorted.

As they parted shortly afterwards Eddie was convinced she must think he was off his head.

The next night he was standing outside her flat, waiting, when she drove round the corner in her old banger of a car. After a coffee they decided to go for a walk on the beach. This time there were no awkward feelings, both knew their friends were praying for them. There, as they walked together on the shore, their relationship moved into a new dimension of warmth and closeness.

Shortly afterwards they became engaged. Eddie shared this exciting piece of news with some young people at an Aberdeen school, when he was asked to give his testimony at one of their lunchtime Scripture Union meetings.

That night Eddie's phone rang. It was the SU leader from the school he had visited, and he had exciting news for Eddie – another unexpected answer to prayer.

'My mother died not long ago,' the man began, 'and she left an engagement ring. I feel the Lord is saying that it would be right for me to give it to you for Leslie.'

An elated Eddie rushed to share the news with his future fiancée. At first she was unsure at the thought of having an old ring, one she hadn't helped to choose. Maybe she wouldn't even like it.

In the event the 'old' ring proved to be a beautiful design of platinum and diamonds. God was giving them something they could never have afforded. What was more, it was the first real ring Eddie had ever offered to a girl.

And it was a perfect fit!

* * * *

Leslie's perspective

My first meeting with Eddie was in my workplace, a Youth Activity Centre where he contributed to a discussion during a 'God Spot'. Later there were formal introductions and Eddie was invited to share his testimony at another 'God Spot'. It didn't stop at formal visits though and Eddie quickly became a regular visitor.

I remember very early on, laying hands on Eddie with a friend during a time of prayer and being disturbed at the pictures that came into my mind. I opened my eyes and mouthed to my friend 'too much for us' as I experienced some of the darkness and turmoil that was part of his life.

Eddie had only been out of prison six months and he was still very raw to the Christian life but nevertheless I look back and realise this should have been a warning sign.

Everything then happened so quickly and there seemed so little space to think. When Eddie and I met for prayer it was after a dilemma. I had to choose between a big Christian Union student party or a down—and—out's meeting and chose the latter. It was a difficult decision as most of my friends were going to the party and there was the added temptation of finding a possible boyfriend! But Eddie was at the meeting and left at the same time as I did, so I offered him a lift in my car.

When he blurted out that he thought God was telling him that I was to be his future wife I was shocked and quite flattered, but knew God could tell me Himself.

I was in a very responsible job and when we

started going out I felt under pressure to keep the relationship 'under wraps' for a while. It is still an issue with Eddie that I refused to hold hands in public. He feels I was embarrassed to go out with an ex–con. The relationship was all–consuming from the very start and Eddie would drop into the workplace all the time but none of us realised how unhealthy it was.

His 'no compromise Christianity' inspired us all and I think it would have been difficult for any of us to forsee the compulsive part which later revealed itself in marriage. Perhaps if the relationship had been slower to develop it might have been easier to see the signs.

5. A marriage made in different worlds

'When your marriage becomes a nightmare what do you do?'

In a way, Eddie had set his sights high. Leslie wasn't just pretty; she shared Eddie's desire to pass on the Gospel and was working with kids from the same sort of background as himself. But going out with Eddie was a different kettle of fish from working with him! They had been brought up in two different worlds and Leslie was ill-prepared for Eddie and Eddie ill-prepared for her. Leslie had a stable family background, a placid temperament and an easy way of forming friendships with both sexes. She was independent and her love of sport and travel had taken her around the world. She had confidence in her own abilities and gifts—in fact the opposite of everything that Eddie had grown up with.

They both believed the relationship was right and many of their friends believed that if anyone could tame Eddie it was Leslie. Sometimes the relationship was such a roller coaster of emotions that there were second thoughts on both sides but friends continued to pray and support them and the two persevered.

The relationship often seemed to be hanging in the balance. One day as the couple walked up Union Street a piece of paper blown by the wind fluttered against their feet and Eddie stopped to pick it up. On the front of the leaflet was a picture of a hand holding a couple together with a Christian message. Eddie felt that God was confirming to them that they should be together but Leslie was still cautious.

Eddie was not a man to hang around and wanted to get married as soon as possible. They had talked and prayed about Eddie's previous marriages, his children and his life in prison and the ups and downs were smoothed over and marriage plans were made. Leslie's parents expressed concern about the speed of the couple's courtship but God's blessing and direction were clearly seen in their lives. A couple of months before they were married,

Eddie's church, Abbey Christian Fellowship, recognised the work Eddie was doing and began to pay him as a full–time evangelist which gave Eddie a sense of direction and purpose.

In the midst of all the planning, and the anticipation of the wedding, there were moments of sheer black comedy when good intentions went disastrously wrong. Eddie, determined to enter marriage fit and healthy, took up weight–lifting and put his back out tripping over one of his own weights only two weeks before the wedding.

On the 25 August 1989 Eddie waited for his bride to arrive. She was late—very, very late. 'She will come won't she?' he asked, overwhelmed with insecurity. Desperate for reassurance his fears were finally relieved by a radiant Leslie making her entrance down the aisle of Gerrard Street Baptist Church. It was a day to remember, as was the honeymoon in Portugal—despite an argument in their first week when Eddie spent ten minutes trying to sleep on a marble floor before going back to bed!

In the very first months of married life, deep-seated problems started to surface. On the work front Eddie was a committed and hard worker. Passionate about his Christian ministry he threw himself into the work and gained widespread admiration and respect.

At home Eddie's behaviour was very hard to handle. It wasn't normal. It wasn't just that he had a quick temper and thought by the 'seat of his pants'. He was illogically jealous and tormented by suspicions that Leslie was ashamed to be seen with an 'ex–con' and nothing she could say would allay his suspicions.

A particular flash point was Leslie's easy conversation with the lads in her workplace. Eddie just could not accept that they weren't chatting her up and he would make life very difficult by making his feelings blatantly obvious with those he saw as a threat.

Few people could have guessed that when he came home he became a different person. Eddie had become so suspicious that he believed that Leslie was seeing someone else. The paranoia developed into irrational behaviour and explosive abuse that was unrelenting and frightening. There were wild outbursts and accusations and Eddie would storm out of the house threatening never to return. He would always come back full of remorse. 'It won't happen again', he would promise. For a while Leslie would accept his apologies and try to reason with him but inevitably it wore her down. The reasoning got her nowhere. Eddie just *couldn't* trust her and because he couldn't trust her he was forever keeping track of where she was, insanely jealous of any tiny suggestion of interest in anyone else. He tested Leslie to the limit, believing that like his first two marriages it was only a matter of time before it ended. If he had a hundred and one reasons for trusting his wife Eddie would find just one which would undermine all his confidence! The marriage made in heaven had turned into a nightmare.

Leslie knew that Eddie desperately needed help but didn't want to broadcast their problems and Eddie had become such an accomplished liar (both inside and outside marriage) that no one really appreciated what Leslie was going through.

It was a downward spiral for Leslie too. One day after an argument, she was physically and emotionally exhausted and began to weep uncontrollably. Eddie knew they both needed help, and rang his pastor.

Douglas had already spent hours trying to get through to Eddie, but felt there were issues that were much deeper. He arranged a weekend at Ellel Grange in Lancashire for Eddie with high hopes that counselling and ministry might provide a real breakthrough. It was soon clear however that Eddie was in denial. Although he went along with the counsellors he was quick to take it all back after each meeting concluded.

Douglas then turned to a counsellor called Roseanne on the West Coast of Scotland. She quickly discovered and confronted Eddie with his habitual lying. She dealt head-on with the problem and there was a measure of healing. Unfortunately before any more work could be done Roseanne's mother died and she was called away to Glasgow and Eddie returned to Aberdeen.

Finally Eddie took a major step and admitted himself to the Royal Cornhill Hospital, demanding treatment, and was referred for a psychologist's report. His report was thoroughly depressing. Eddie's symptoms – his unreasonable belief that Leslie was unfaithful, his displays of extreme jealousy and his constant cross-examination of Leslie's whereabouts

— were a perfect description of 'pathological jealousy'.

At the time it seemed like a hopeless situation. Medically speaking Eddie had a serious condition that was hard to treat. Counselling wasn't working and the breakthrough that everyone had hoped for seemed to be a long way away.

It was almost a relief to know that there was a real medical problem. But it meant coming to terms with some hard and frightening facts. Eddie's personality disorder stemmed from a lifetime of low self—esteem. It could, Leslie was warned, lead to violent attacks on the sexual partner and in some cases murder. It was the psychologist's professional opinion that complete cure was unlikely. The news was hardly comforting.

Inevitably others saw the downward spiral of abuse. Jackie, one of Leslie's friends, and Douglas the pastor, witnessed one violent outburst in full swing. Eddie pulled a kitchen knife from the drawer and threatened to kill himself.

Friends of Eddie and Leslie could now see the enormity of the problem. It wasn't that Eddie didn't love Leslie—quite the opposite. It wasn't that Leslie had given Eddie any grounds for suspicion. The real problems lay a long way back. More than anything else, Eddie's early years – his sense of inadequacy and insecurity, years of feeling unwanted – were now taking their toll on his marriage. He desperately wanted to make things work and yet however hard he tried, he was hurting those he loved most.

In a normal person, being overwhelmed with negative feelings is part of the stress and grief of life–changing events and is overcome through time and common sense. What was happening to Eddie was that his 'morbidity' had become an ever–present stream of consciousness in the mind, a sort of whirlpool taking on a life of its own. Common sense and rational argument couldn't break in.

What could be done? Leslie had clearly reached breaking point. It was suggested they should separate for at least two months until Eddie got some more counselling help.

It was a difficult situation. Eddie moved back to his mother's and agreed to take the pressure off by attending a Brethren Assembly whilst Leslie continued going to the Abbey Fellowship. Meanwhile Eddie's friends had the unshakeable belief that God could heal through prayer.

A ray of hope

Mike and Jan Wendes seemed vastly unsuited to tackling Eddie. 'Eddie will eat them for breakfast,' Leslie said dismissively. They were a young, 'laid-back' couple that led a house group Bible study and had willingly agreed to work with Eddie. Leslie thought their services would be very short–lived!

Although Eddie had moved back with his mother, that hadn't stopped him making a nuisance of himself. He phoned or called on Leslie regularly, still wanting reassurance that the separation was only temporary. At first Leslie was just relieved that his visits weren't aggressive but after a while she just wanted peace. 'Stop contacting me—if you change I'll see it and you won't need to tell me,' she told him angrily. 'Leave me alone!' Once she met him in a car park and it was pitiful to see how deeply he longed for the marriage to be restored but Leslie couldn't face the future at that point.

Surprisingly Mike and Jan built up a good relationship with Eddie and gradually he began to share with them the hurts and bitterness of his past life. As the bitterness poured out so the work of prayer began to heal and restore. Those who were involved in working and praying for Eddie could see real evidence that the aggressive, hard Eddie was becoming much softer and more sensitive to others' needs.

Whilst Eddie was struggling with his negative feelings and the abuse he had inflicted, Leslie was attempting to pick up the pieces. She was exhausted mentally and emotionally by the months of trauma. She struggled to see God's purpose in her pain. Why had he allowed all this to happen to one of his children? She felt spiritually numb—could she trust God to get things right? She couldn't pray properly, couldn't read her Bible. She felt she had nothing left.

Leslie needed as much healing time as Eddie. It took many weeks before she could even begin to come to terms with what had happened. A close friend gave her a copy of the book, *From Prison to Praise,* by Merlin Carothers, which encouraged her to thank God for the bad times as well as the good. Gradually some of the hardness and bitterness began to go and she felt able to claim for herself the Bible verse: 'Be joyful always; pray continually; give thanks in all circumstances, for this is God's will for you in Christ Jesus' (1 Thess. 5: 16).

Leslie began to see a glimmer of light at the end of the tunnel. She regained a measure of independence and re–discovered her old enjoyment of sport. But in the background Eddie still lurked and she dreaded the moment when friends might suggest possible reconciliation.

'Give Eddie another chance'

'I want you to give Eddie another chance,' Leslie's pastor told her. A tidal wave of emotions hit and overwhelmed her and the battle raged. Reason told her that it was impossible to re–build her marriage as she feared Eddie could suffocate and overwhelm her.

What was God telling her to do? 'Surely you're not going to make me go through all this again, Father?' she prayed. 'I can't trust him. I don't think he'll ever change.' But she also knew that God intended marriage to be a lifetime commitment and if others saw hope for a renewed relationship she needed to trust their judgment and face this new ordeal.

It was very clear that Eddie accepted the marriage could only work under new terms and conditions and that he needed to be a changed character. The Wendes were ready to support, encourage and monitor steps towards reconciliation and Leslie felt secure from that point of view.

Leslie felt it was much against her better judgment when she agreed to a first low–key meeting with Eddie at the Wendes' home. But then neither had any idea that they were keeping a divine appointment.

The Wendes had worked hard to bring the two together but it didn't make the first meeting any easier. Leslie sat on the sofa keeping her eyes fixed on her feet wondering what was going to happen.

The Wendes began with prayer and then played a track of a worship tape. Don Francisco sang the words:

> *I could never promise you on just my strength alone*
> *That all my life I'd care for you and love you as my own,*
> *I'd never know the future, I only see today*
> *Words that last a lifetime would be more than I could say.*
> *But the love inside my heart today is more than mine alone.*
> *It never changes, it never fails, it never seeks its own*

*And by the God who gives it and who lives in me
  and you
Know the words I speak to you today are words I'm
  going to do.
So I stand before you now for all to hear and see
And promise you in Jesus' Name, the love He's given
  me
And through the years on earth and as eternity
  goes by
The life and love he's given us are never going to
  die.*

'I could never promise you on just my strength alone…' There was stunned silence and then tears began to course down Leslie's face. She dared not look up but sensed that Eddie had left the room. An overwhelming sense of God's presence filled the room as they heard the song that had been sung at their wedding and that the Wendes, unaware of its significance, had been prompted to choose.

For the first time Eddie felt relief. He realised that God was telling him that he wasn't in the driving seat and that God was in control. Eddie wasn't to rely on his own strength but, praise God, change by His strength was possible.

Every week the supervised meetings

continued and slowly confidence grew. Leslie began to collect Eddie from his mother's house and drive him to the Wendes where they talked and prayed. It took a while longer before they felt able to sit beside each other and still longer before they reached the momentous point of holding hands.

After five months separation Leslie agreed to Eddie returning. It wasn't plain sailing! There were troubled months and times when Eddie seemed to make progress and then fall back into bad habits. This time, however, Eddie and Leslie had a team of people who knew the score and were ready to pray and work together as a team to support them. The marriage was back on track—repaired by a Redeemer-Saviour at work through His people.

Eddie and Leslie have had their ups and downs since but their marriage problems are well and truly behind them. The journey back hasn't been easy or fast but they can testify that the long haul was worth it.

Eddie knows that he has been a nightmare to live with and he is ashamed of what Leslie has had to go through. But he also knows that he is forgiven and believes that whatever the consequences of a bad life, God, through the work of the Holy Spirit, can change us and help us to see ourselves as we really are. He is the One who is faithful and who is able to give us honesty to talk, openness to listen, love to share, power to persevere.

On Sunday 25 August 2002 Eddie and Leslie celebrated their thirteenth wedding anniversary. Both sent cards to each other with one single red rose on the front.

Eddie's card to Leslie was a poignant 'thank you' for 'hanging in there' and for having three lovely children. 'You couldn't have known what a long haul it would be,' Eddie continued, 'but what is now built is so valuable.'

Leslie's card read: 'If at first you don't succeed, try it your wife's way!'

It says a great deal about their marriage, that they can laugh at the past.

* * * *

Leslie's perspective

Looking back, Eddie and I had such different outlooks on life and there was a massive gap. Eddie had no grey areas—everything had to be black or white.

After we married it quickly became apparent that Eddie didn't find it easy to adapt to the daily routine and objected to my work responsibilities. Working evenings became a problem as Eddie didn't like being in on his own and our 'roles' became an issue. Often Eddie would arrive before the end of my shift to take me home or to come and participate in the evening. At other times I was very aware that Eddie was checking up on me, wanting to know my whereabouts or even following me to double check.

Eddie's unpredictability and the way he could distort and twist things was alarming. I remember one afternoon whilst I was ironing, asking Eddie what had become of 'Racy'. Racy was an alcoholic 'down and out' that we both worked with. I didn't expect the violent accusation of 'You fancy him' and the outburst that followed.

Eddie's outbursts were becoming a regular occurrence and I spent hours reasoning with him. Afterwards he would make fresh and pitiful demands. 'Do you love me?' 'How much do you love me?' It was exhausting having to work through the confrontations and then become a loving comforter. I knew that none of the issues were resolved.

I didn't have the experience to understand how deep—seated the problems were and the more Eddie applied the pressure the more desperate I became for space to cope.

After fourteen months of marriage and trying to work through issues without success I realised that Eddie's idea of love was based entirely on feelings. Because the feelings were not founded in an act of will they were totally distorted and I realised it was hopeless. There seemed to be no-one who could help and I was increasingly worn down physically and emotionally. When he was diagnosed at Cornhill I was advised that there was also the whole issue of my safety.

Once Eddie had moved out he was told by the elders to give me breathing space and they insisted on rules to safeguard me. Eddie had to give up his OFTAN job too and for a while was heavily doped up and referred to a Christian psychologist.

I felt really angry. I didn't know who I was any more and my confidence was crushed. Eventually crying, anger and bitterness ran their course and God gave me a period of re–affirmation and forgiveness. I was able to say 'give thanks in all circumstances.'

6. Loser!

*'Will I ever prove
that I'm good enough?'*

It wasn't just Eddie's marriage that needed sorting out. One of the ways that Eddie needed to change was to demonstrate he could take responsibility in day-to-day work. All his desires to serve the Lord in the work of the ministry had to be set to one side and Eddie had to prove to himself, to Leslie and the world that he could hold down a job.

Over a seven year period Eddie proved that he wasn't a loser but had gained respect and recognition—but like his marriage it didn't all come easily.

Facing up to failure
When Eddie and Leslie's marriage fell apart

so did Eddie's ministry. 'It's not right' Eddie protested when the pastor told him that he could no longer continue with his full time ministry until he got sorted out.

The bottom dropped out of Eddie's world. Not only was his marriage a failure but having his work taken from him was a deep blow to Eddie's pride. He loved his work and it had been, in his words, 'going on great'. He was well-respected and liked. The church had even offered him the job of Assistant Pastor. Did it have to finish just because he was 'cracking up' with Leslie?

Being in ministry was the only thing Eddie wanted to do. When he was offered the position of Assistant Pastor his ego soared. He had always felt a bit envious of Leslie's work and was proud of his promotion.

His mind told him that the decision to step down was right but his heart told him very differently. He lost his head totally when he visited the church offices one day to pick up his wages and found a replacement at his desk. Anger welled up and jealousy overwhelmed him. He lost control and lashed out and punched the man in the face. The man reeled back, disorientated by the blow and vulnerable without his smashed glasses. Eddie wasn't repentant! He did, however, realise that his anger had got the better of him.

His pastor took the incident very seriously and involved an off–duty Christian policeman who confronted Eddie in no uncertain terms and told him that compensation was due for the broken glasses.

Eddie knew deep down that his aggressive action wouldn't restore the past and that he needed to deal with his problems but he was engulfed in his own misery. He safeguarded himself where possible by lying and hugged his pain and hurt to himself. He even wondered if it was worth having God in his life if He couldn't instantly restore his marriage. Had God deserted him like all the others?

Finding work gave Eddie some focus—a night-time job cleaning helicopters and a part-time day job as a hospital cleaner.

His marriage had broken up in September 1990 and his first Christmas without Leslie seemed particularly hard. He was living with his mother Muriel and his brother and on Christmas Eve things came to a head. Eddie turned to his brother, his face a picture of misery. 'Do you think I'm gonna make it? All I can see is I've blown it twice, I've got kids [from a previous marriage]... I just canna see it working.'

Eddie's brother was impatient with the continual problems and encouraged Eddie to drown his sorrows. 'C'mon Eddie, let's go for a bevvie. It's no good moping about here.'

But Eddie wasn't interested. Bitterness and anger consumed him. He had lost his job and his marriage. Being rejected again he couldn't cope. Aggression was his defence. He sat slumped in his chair with Ian White's praise and worship music playing and tears rolled down his cheeks. 'I canna take any more of this,' he thought, and went to the bathroom for a razor blade. With the razor blade in his hand he struggled to think some sense. His mind screamed out, 'End it!' In the midst of all his confusion there was a sudden sense of God's presence and peace. He felt able to pray, 'Lord, if my marriage goes down, ah'm still going to put you first in ma life.' His prayer was a small chink of light that signalled progress.

By the following Christmas, Eddie was not only back with Leslie but had his first taste of full–time work in a joiner's shop.

At that point the couple were enabled to get a mortgage and move from Leslie's flat to their first home in Donview Road in Aberdeen.

Eddie then applied to the railways as a trackman. Ex–offenders weren't supposed to get jobs but he filled in the application form anyway, gained an interview, passed a medical and was offered the job.

The job suited him. He enjoyed being physically tired and getting out of bed at 6.00am to have a prayer time before arriving at work at 7.00am—an hour early!

The job was essentially maintenance of the lines; ten days followed by a night shift. Some days they would be rebuilding lines, other times walking from Portlethen right into Aberdeen checking the lines or driving as far down as Dundee for work.

The first crisis came within a year, but it was none of Eddie's doing. One night some builders broke into the office, got into the safe and stole goods, including a microwave. When Eddie heard the news he thought his job would be gone for sure and awaited a visit from the CID. It was no surprise to him to be summoned to the office the following morning. But he didn't anticipate what he was about to hear. 'You're the only guy we can trust—would you think about becoming a leading trackman?'

What an encouragement! Eddie's boss saw some good in him even if the church couldn't see it! Eddie was still insecure and raw inside. The thing that really got to him was that God had saved him, made him a 'good boy' but he was prevented from leadership because of his marriage problems and yet at work they could see his leadership potential.

Eddie was overflowing with a love and compassion for his fellow workers that at times overwhelmed him. The trackmen were a rough and ready group and Eddie was quick to challenge them with the Gospel. The men enjoyed a good bevvie and the usual camaraderie of dirty jokes whilst Eddie was labelled 'middle–class' for not joining in. Some would come and offload their problems in the darkness of the night shift and two mates even came to church to hear him speak—one of the few times Eddie had the opportunity. He couldn't help but feel his place was in the ministry.

Eddie's squad made its mark very early on.

It was a beautiful day and there were five of them working on the line with 'Kanga' Guns—big vibrating machines that pack and compact stones under the sleepers. Unbeknown to the squad a train was proceeding up the track at 100 miles an hour and the squad further up the line were signalling like crazy its approach. At exactly the wrong moment, the squad's lookout chose to take his orange safety vest off to remove his Celtic shirt. Everyone was wearing earmuff protectors and Eddie sensed rather than heard the approach and pushed the others, screaming a warning. Five men dived off the track as the train (which had started its braking mechanisms nearly a mile back) screamed to a halt some way past them. There was a chorus of 'phut, phut, phut' as the air-conditioned hoses were severed. Later five red faces in the squad faced the implications of their very near miss.

Another episode was an even closer shave and one in which Eddie knows God kept him safe. There was an incident in Portlethen in which there had been a derailment with wooden carriages. The squad had to lift the line with a 'horse' (a piece of machinery with clamps designed for the job). As the ton weight of rail was swung across, Eddie guided it into position putting his weight underneath the rail. Disaster struck. Eddie slipped and (as he saw in slow motion) the rail came down directly over his arm. There was a dull thump as the rail contacted with the ground but miraculously Eddie's arm had found a hollow and he was able to pull his hand out from underneath. It was bruised and cut and he had to have it in a sling and checked out at the hospital but his mates knew that it should have been crushed! Eddie remembers the journey to hospital because the driver insisted on stopping in a Forestry Commission copse, taking a saw to a Christmas tree and delivering it to his wife and children, before taking Eddie to Casualty.

Another responsibility Eddie was given was to drive the squad to location. As he remembers, it wasn't all hard work. On night shifts they had a portable television and used to catch up on the 'fitba'. There was one night when it had snowed very heavily and there were great drifts on the line. The squad had been watching TV but like great kids had taken delight in the snow and were using their snow shovels to sledge when a warning was suddenly shouted that the boss was on his way. Eddie will never forget his boss jumping over the railway fence and disappearing totally in deep snow and the men scrabbling to the truck to hide the TV!

It was in this job that Eddie really began to find his feet. Initially he felt that he had lost much of his physical as well as emotional strength and there were still times when he felt suicidal. But Eddie didn't realise that he needed breaking down and that he needed breaking more than once! God wanted to break Eddie's attitude of wanting prestige and power and working as a trackman was part of a much bigger picture. It certainly wasn't a glamorous job—with orange boiler suit and 'sweetie money' pay, and forced to go back to the classroom to take courses involving maths (to work out speeds, cants and slants), lifting techniques, Health and Safety procedures and First Aid issues. It proved to Eddie that he *could* learn. Not bad for a man that couldn't read whilst he was in prison!

Despite Eddie's low self esteem, he was determined to prove himself. The more he learnt the more he realised just how much there was to learn. One day he shared with his classmates that he was embarrassed when he went to church and discovered he couldn't even say 'good morning' to the people in front of him because they were deaf and dumb. 'So,' he said, 'I did away and learnt a bit of sign language.' His evident abilities and determination were noted as 'leadership potential'.

Determination opened doors at work but it didn't work at church. He still wasn't 'good enough' for leadership until he realised that God wanted him to 'die to self' and allow a work of instruction and teaching in his life. Nevertheless Eddie never lost the certainty in his seven years of secular work that God was calling him to serve. While he was working on the railways he said to Leslie, pointing at his heart, 'I've got a thing here. It's not of the flesh; it's not disappearing. I've got a thing here that God's got a purpose for me'.

Whilst on the railways, Eddie befriended a woman called Mhairi who came to the church and heard his testimony. Now in her thirties, she had a long history of petty crime. For Mhairi, setting fire to phone boxes and regularly cutting herself was a cry for help. She had little education but she would sit in the meetings sucking her thumb and listening to Eddie.

When Eddie spoke of his heavenly Father's love Mhairi would become very distressed. As trust was built she was able to tell him that from the age of six her father had sexually abused her and she was overwhelmed by a sense of guilt and dirtiness.

Eddie persuaded Mhairi to go to the police and they requested Eddie to accompany her to make a statement because 'she trusts you'. In his heart of hearts he knew that what he wanted to do most of all was to help hurting people overcome their circumstances and find true freedom through the love of Jesus.

He still sees Mhairi. She has become a Christian although she finds friendships and church–going hard to sustain. But she hasn't cut herself for a long time now and is reducing her medication. She feels she is in control of her life.

After several years on the railways, privatisation changed the structure of Eddie's job and he felt it was time for a change. He got a job as a 'brickie' for a couple of years to learn new skills and revelled in new physical challenges. Of course he couldn't help but treat every building site as a fresh parish for preaching and sometimes came in for criticism because he spent too long talking about God!

There were always workmates who used to bring their *piece* (lunch) and sit round for a regular dose of his stories. On one building site Eddie got involved with a 'sparkie' who deliberately wired up his house to electrocute his family. His reign of terror was eventually uncovered and he was put away, but his family will be permanently traumatised.

Another man Eddie met was a huge Casanova of a fellow, Andrew, who had a weakness for women but had a lovely wife at home. He was greatly challenged by coming to church and hearing Eddie's testimony and broke down but the following day admitted he was about to walk out on his wife and run off with another woman. His defence against his guilty conscience was to build up anger and self–righteousness. That week there was a 'jumped–up' foreman on site that got under everyone's skin, 'swanning around' and making life difficult—so much so that, in blind anger, Andrew decided that the foreman would be buried in concrete. Eddie had no doubts whatsoever that he meant it and stuck to Andrew like glue. For that week he became his conscience until they moved sites and the danger was past. Shortly after, Andrew left his wife for another woman.

An open door

After seven years God gave Eddie the open door into the work he so much desired. Although Eddie hated being branded 'the ex con' and sometimes felt used he often told his story. He knew it was for God's glory, but he wanted to do more than just talk about his past.

At this point several things happened. Teen Challenge, an international organisation working with drug addicts and prostitutes (with an office based in Edinburgh), suggested that Eddie might work with them. They had the policy of employing people who 'lived by faith' but Eddie felt it right that he should be offered a salary and would only accept a funded place. Teen Challenge after some discussion accepted the terms but on the condition that they could raise the funds.

Meanwhile Eddie was asked to speak at Eden Court Theatre, Inverness, sharing the platform with Chuck Colson, notorious for his involvement in the American Watergate scandal and now devoted to prison work. The privilege of addressing 2,500 people and testifying to what God had done for him moved Eddie to tears. Shortly after he was invited to address another large meeting organised by the Edinburgh Men's Christian Fellowship and after the meeting was approached by Prison Fellowship Scotland with the view to possible employment.

The interview with Prison Fellowship Scotland went well and Eddie was offered a job as a Prison Worker, whilst the possibility of work with Teen Challenge didn't materialise. Eddie was clear about the direction that God wanted him to take.

Seven years seemed a long time but Eddie realises now that he needed to prove he could 'walk worthy' and although at first he felt resentful and bitter and often frustrated because he was eager to move on, he also learned to submit to God's timing.

The lesson is clear. For those who have failed, be encouraged. God knows your longings and frustrations. He also knows the length of time needed in preperation to move on and times it perfectly. Eddie can testify that the long wait was worth it as he faced a new beginning.

*Part Three:
Restoring the Years*

7. New beginnings

' Still learning?'

Eddie was on a six month trial. He was determined to prove himself in his new job and he set about it with 100 percent commitment. He hadn't got a 'fancy education' but he had got life experience, and he reckoned that was every bit as good.

Vivid memories

It was an eventful six months and Eddie started with his home city, Aberdeen, and a tour of a prison that he knew very well—Craiginches.

His first day was very strange. He was returning to the prison in which he had spent several years of his life and he felt just like a fish out of water, sitting at the Governor's table with tea, coffee, and sandwiches discussing how best they could support the prisoners. It just didn't seem real.

But when the Governor took him on a tour of the prison it broke Eddie down. The cold reality hit him. There were people he knew still there—people who had re-offended and were still acting like twenty-one-year-olds, still running about with hand-guns, doing crazy stuff.

Eddie was given complete freedom—in fact he was being shown around as though he had never been there before! As they opened each new area Eddie saw old faces.

Catching up with the past

He remembered Jimmy only too well. He could picture the scene back then: with two others sitting on the stairs, in shorts with towels around their waists. Dressed like that they could stab a guy then nip straight into the showers. Jimmy had been 'tooled up' with a knife made out of a screwdriver and he was planning to do as much damage to Eddie as he could as punishment for not bringing drugs back in, after a weekend pass.

'Hey! Eddie Murison! Your life's changed, innit? Ey, you made it, ain't you?' Jimmy came over to talk to the group of men. 'But what about you guys? You can make it too,' Eddie replied. It was reassuring that the inmates knew he was a changed man. They could *see* he had changed all right. Some of the inmates argued with him: 'You've changed sides noo, you're management, we canna trust you.' But Eddie could testify: 'What I am is hope for you guys, evidence that your lives can change too.'

The 'sheds' brought back vivid memories. Here the men worked like zombies, making nets with needle and stick. It is different today, but then it was tedious work with little opportunity for breaks. Eddie remembered his violent outbreak in the sheds with shame. He had used a head—height iron bar used for making army camouflage nets to smash the glass screen dividers that ran the length of the shed. He reduced the prison to absolute chaos that day and was so violent he needed to be protected from himself.

He wasn't the only one who remembered. One of the prison officers was still there and was stunned at the change that he saw in Eddie.

Threats

Eddie only had to make two visits to the Craiginches prison, where he was allowed 'walkabout'. Trouble was to come. The inmates had spotted the potential to bring drugs into the prison and targeted Eddie. He was dropping off the children at nursery when he was approached by three men, who threatened him with, 'If you don't take drugs in, your family is going to be damaged.'

He didn't know what to do or how to tell Leslie. She was pregnant with their third child and the last thing he wanted to do was worry her. They were packing up the house to move to Perth. He didn't know what to do, even being tempted for a moment to give in.

A day or so later they were on the seafront at Johnshaven when Fiona (their oldest) yelled 'Big Whalie!' She had spotted a school of dolphins, the first Eddie had ever seen. As they watched this wonderful sight of them twisting and looping in the water, Eddie confided in Leslie. 'That explains the red car crawling past our house,' she said slowly. She remembered wondering why the occupants had all turned and looked directly into their house windows.

Leslie went very quiet. 'Promise me Eddie', she said, 'If anything happens to me or the kids, that you won't damage anyone, but pray it through.' The challenge reduced Eddie to tears.

Although Eddie and Leslie were shortly to move to a more central location in Perth, a Prison Fellowship trustee was very worried by the threats and asked that Eddie and his family move into his Glasgow house for a while. But Eddie wasn't going to take threats lying down. The following day he phoned up the Prison Service at Craiginches and spoke to the Governor. 'We're moving to Perth soon but we're under pressure to take drugs in,' he explained. 'Could you insist on strip searching me when I go in?'

The Project Manager took the threats very seriously and he and the prison management gave Eddie tremendous support so that the next time Eddie went in he had an uncompromising message for the inmates: 'I've been saved from the bondage of fear,' he said. 'I'm not going to be controlled by you muppets.' His words seemed to release others and numbers at Sunday meetings swelled from three inmates to forty men, with some making serious commitments.

How can I get money?

It was at Craiginches that Eddie met Sandy, a country boy from Elgin. There were about twenty inmates at the Bible Study and Eddie was talking about God's love and how God could support them inside or out. Sandy broke down and wept. He was on the point of being released and he dreaded facing his life outside. 'I've got five kids, I'm no living with my wife, I've a girlfriend with a kid. How can I support them? I'm an ex-junkie. How can I get money?' Eddie heard the pressure in his voice and his heart went out to this hard man reduced to tears. He got up from his chair and reached out for the man and gave him 'such a cuddle'. They wept together, Eddie telling him that God loved him and knew and cared about his difficulties.

There was a strange quiet in the room as the other men put their heads down. In a male prison feelings are rarely on display but the men knew that what was happening was real and they were moved. At the end of the meeting fifteen out of the twenty men asked for prayer.

Wife-beating

It wasn't just the inmates who were moved.

118

There was one prison officer who repeatedly listened and was deeply affected by what he heard. One day just as Eddie was finishing the meeting the officer asked if he could have a 'quick word' and in the corridor asked if he might visit Eddie's home.

The following day he was on Eddie's doorstep asking Eddie if God could help him. He told Eddie that there were some inmates who were at Craiginches as the result of wife–battering. 'I've to lock these men away and then I go to the pub, get drunk and then I go home and beat my wife. Can anyone help me with my marriage?' he asked shamefaced. Eddie asked a Christian ex–prison officer to come alongside to counsel the officer.

The big move

Just over a year after Eddie started work with Prison Fellowship Scotland, the family moved. Whilst Eddie and Leslie had the upheaval of looking at houses and changing schools, Eddie was doing a whistle–stop tour of the Scottish prison system introducing himself to management as the new Prison Fellowship Scotland Worker. A roadshow was then organised throughout the towns and cities of Scotland.

The move was good timing. Eddie and Leslie had changed a good deal and had grown in confidence, matured spiritually and were enjoying life as a family unit. Their move to Perth gave them the opportunity to prove that they could be independent of the practical day–to–day support of their Aberdeen church. In some ways it was a lonely time and because they had little support, but they felt they had to trust God in simply everything.

Moving into Perth was stressful but even more so because Eddie and Leslie were moving into the unknown. They knew that the move was right but there were so many things to think about. They had to think carefully about what they could afford. The house they found was on a hillside overlooking Perth and Friarton Prison, with a stunning view of the Ochils beyond. Buying the house was one thing but carpets and other practicalities were another. As they prayed they thanked God for every provision He provided. Money was given for built–in wardrobes and carpets. Someone even donated a conservatory—Eddie used his 'brickie' skills and erected it himself. It became his prayer and snooze place (when he could keep the rest of the family out of it!).

Another problem was lack of space for an office. Always practical, Eddie was working in the attic, resting his weight on a few chipboard squares scattered across the rafters. There were answers to prayer on that score too, and the money was provided – enough for the flooring and plasterboard walls, doors and lighting.

Sometimes as Eddie was preaching and speaking on behalf of Prison Fellowship he would be given practical gifts. Often it seemed that the Lord knew just what to lay on peoples' hearts to give and when. One day Eddie was presented with a salmon 'as big as his arm' (a treat that they would never have bought). It was perfect for the special church lunch that followed the dedication of their third child, Stuart.

The accident

There were too many things happening in those first few months, and not surprisingly Eddie got very tired. One Sunday morning he was travelling from Glen Ochil Prison on his way to Glasgow in his old banger of a car – which had broken down more times than he cared to remember—when for a split second Eddie fell asleep at the wheel and the car swung out of control.

How long he was unconscious he doesn't know. When he re-opened his eyes he discovered he was strapped from head to foot to his seat. A policemen was scanning his mobile for a contact phone number. 'We're trying to find out who you are,' the policeman said, and handed it back to him, along with his Bible which was on the back seat. 'You might need this,' the policeman said.

Eddie was terrified! He was strapped down so that he couldn't move and worried about the weight of his legs. When they took him into x-ray for the first time and questioned the results he became even more agitated. 'There seems to be a bone sticking out in your neck,' they said. 'Can you tell us if it is an old wound?' That was enough to get Eddie thoroughly wound up. Worse still, he didn't know why Leslie wasn't there and (as she was heavily pregnant) thought she might have gone into labour. 'I'm not accepting this, Lord,' he prayed. 'There's no way I'm going to be driven about. I want to run about and tell people what you've done for me. You've set me free, Lord! You can do it again!'

Meanwhile Leslie had been visiting a friend in Dumfries and was told to stay put, awaiting news. It was a worrying time but when the x-rays came back the second time round the mysterious bone was nowhere to be found! Eddie had seen quite enough of hospitals for one day, and dressed and discharged himself before anyone could protest too much.

The first thing he did was collect his car. It looked comparatively undamaged but the impact had twisted and concertinaed the subframe badly. The police told him he was lucky that he had escaped with so little injury. Eddie handed the PC a copy of his book, *Bruised but not broken,* and explained that in this case he had been 'bruised but not broken'!

The slow tour

After the tour of the prisons Eddie got involved in his first project. Prison Fellowship acquired an old double-decker bus from a Christian organisation in Aberdeen, to travel the length and breadth of Scotland, visiting towns and cities. There was so much bad publicity about Scotland's prisons that Eddie wanted the bus to be a public relations exercise in which he and a volunteer force could tell others about the positive effects of the Christian message in Her

123

Majesty's Prisons. Eddie wanted the bus to go on tour for a month. But it was agreed that two weeks was a good start and it proved to be a great success. It was the first experiment of its kind and the bus was parked in city centres and an amazing number of people came on board. There were evangelistic meetings organised, along with street work and visits to prisons.

In Dundee two young teenagers boarded the bus. It was obvious that they were skiving school and didn't want to go home. Eddie believes if only for these two youngsters the tour was worthwhile as the two admitted that their mother's boyfriend was sexually abusing them. As a result the conversation was followed up by the Police and Social Work Department.

In Aberdeen a woman in her sixties attended the evening meeting in a local Church of Scotland where Eddie was speaking and told him: 'My son was involved in drink and drugs and with the help of Prison Fellowship he has been set free.' With tears of joy she finished by saying 'I've got my son back and he's now able to work full time.' She wasn't the only one with tears in her eyes—it was a joy to see results from the ministry.

Another of the encouragements of the tour was the unity and compassion that came out of it. More than once Eddie worked with Christian policemen and prison officers. Off-duty (wearing jeans and jackets and therefore unrecognised) they would take money out of their back pockets and give to an inmate's wife because they knew and understood the frustrations at first hand.

Eddie shared this story later in Perth Prison. In the corner of the room was a prison officer and as Eddie spoke of the love demonstrated by Christian Prison Officers the man broke down. There were tears running down Eddie's face as he heard this prison officer respond. He looked up and the hardened criminals and lifers who were Christians had tears running down their faces too. There was a powerful sense of God's presence in the room, a realisation that God was working in men's lives. This was Eddie's first encouragement from a prison officer and as the meeting turned to prayer the officer said, 'If this is the sort of God that makes people act like this, I want Him in my life too.' 'Something happened that night—that was powerful stuff,' said the chaplain.

Another practical outworking of the Roadshow was the recruitment of volunteers for Drop-in Centres, which is how the Centre in Inverness began.

The bus definitely had its down sides however—breakdowns were the main one! At one point this drove them almost to despair. They had a roadshow organised in Inverness but the bus would not move. Eddie sent out volunteers to look for a lorry, caravan, anything that would hold the equipment whilst he looked for a suitable mechanic. Eventually the bus functioned again but only at a top speed of twenty mph, at which speed they crawled into Inverness arriving in the early hours of the morning. They had 'can't miss it' directions for their Bed and Breakfast accommodation—a certain street and a house with a red car outside. With no less than three B&B houses with red cars, they decided that whichever house had an open front door that was the one in which they were going to sleep.

Thankfully it was the right house they chose and they were to be half–woken the next morning by puzzled conversation in the hall. The bus was parked outside but where were the occupants? It took them a few minutes to discover the slumbering bodies in the living room!

The Roadshow heralded the end of Eddie's first year with Prison Fellowship Scotland and already he was beginning to find his feet. What would the Lord have in store for him next?

8. Life in the raw

*'When your job seems to be all
'downs', can you survive?*

As Eddie got into the day–to–day workload he often examined his own life. He was constantly amazed at how much he had changed. The light that had penetrated his own darkness had also dealt with the pain, violence and anger which had been part of him. The real prison bars had been broken and he was no longer struggling with hatred and desperation. He knew he was no longer the same as the inmates but was a new creation. It never failed to surprise him especially when he came across difficulties and was able to control himself without using his fists! The prison staff found it equally strange. They were encouraged that they weren't just meeting a changed man, but a new man. The

Bible describes it exactly: 'Therefore, if anyone is in Christ, he is a new creation; the old has gone, the new has come!' (2 Cor. 5:17).

Eddie found himself doing all sorts of jobs in his first six months. But he never lost sight of the importance of demonstrating that Christ is the only one who can answer human need. He delighted in bringing the message of the Bible to prisoners, and wanted to show how relevant it was to their lives. He would often use Bible stories of people that had been messed up by power, adultery, lies, corruption, drink or greed to show that human nature hasn't changed. He would then explain the wonderful change that new life in Christ makes, and how it changes people from the inside out—giving new hopes, new attitudes, new freedom.

As trust between Eddie and prisoners became established he found himself getting involved with prisoners' families. Prisoners trusted him to sort out problems in their private lives. They expected him to treat their problems in confidence and this became a major part of Eddie's ministry. It was amazing to him that the people that would formerly have shunned him and kept a safe distance now came to unburden themselves and to treat him as their 'Agony Uncle'!

Facing death

Eddie faced 'ups' and terrible 'downs' in his work. One of the downsides of the ministry was the funerals—men who couldn't face life, simply gave up and committed suicide. In the first year, Eddie attended twenty-five funerals. Often these were people with whom he had become very close and their deaths were bitter personal blows. He felt that these men had been offered hope for the future and some had come so near and yet were so far.

Ewan Sinclair was only a young man of seventeen when Eddie met him huddled in a corner seat of a Burger King. Eddie sat next to him and handed him a steaming mug of coffee and an assorted plate of sugary doughnuts. It was a dark night and the window clearly reflected Ewan as he cautiously worked his way through the feast. Eddie watched the reflection of his hands picking up one doughnut after another.

Abruptly Ewan stopped eating, straightened up and said 'How long will it be before you reject me?'

'What do you mean?' said Eddie

Ewan started to tell Eddie about himself. At the age of five his mum had run away with her boyfriend to England, leaving Ewan with an alcoholic father. Eventually Ewan was referred to the Social Work Department. 'I've been in care, nobody can cope with me, nobody cares and you're just the same,' he said dismissively.

It was then that Eddie was able to tell Ewan a bit about himself—about his own rejection and insecurity. In turn Ewan felt able to tell Eddie that he had been sexually abused by different people, and bullied.

Eddie could feel the hurt and his heart went out to the young man. 'If you really want help,' he suggested, 'I can take you to a place in Dornoch. You can be part of a family and a church fellowship where people *do* care and will be supportive.'

Eddie was thrilled when Ewan took up the offer. But all did not go as well as Eddie had hoped. Ewan was deeply insecure in his new environment and determined to test his new friends to their limits. He couldn't grasp the notion that the love he was experiencing was unconditional. He was determined to prove that it 'had strings attached'. He made life very difficult indeed, determined to manipulate any rule going! Everything was an issue and every issue he wanted to control. The fellowship was stretched to the limits as Ewan played one family off against another.

One day Ewan received a cheque for £100 from an Aberdonian policeman who wanted to give him the opportunity for a fresh start, to dispose of any stolen goods and to buy himself clothes.

It was all too much. He could not accept the situation and things came to a head. Eddie was asked to come and sort him out. Realising the urgency he got into the car and drove as fast as he could. He arrived at the tiny house in Dornoch, leapt the wall and entered the house without knocking. He pounded up the stairs, leaving a trail of mud prints on the stair carpet (how was he to know about the boggy pool on the other side of the wall?) and burst, without ceremony, into Ewan's bedroom.

He felt decidedly short-tempered as he faced this young man. 'Before you say anything' said Ewan, 'see this dog?' He was lying on his bed cuddling a sheepdog. 'He won't bark at me, won't bite me, won't criticise me. I can trust him. I can't trust people.'

Realising that the situation wasn't going to work Eddie came up with another proposal. 'Ewan, come nine o'clock next morning I'm taking you back—we've got a job for you.'

Even the journey back was difficult. Ewan was determined to provoke Eddie. 'I'm just a case to you, you don't really care,' he kept saying. Eddie's patience was wearing very thin and he braked sharply to a standstill and pulled into the side of the road. 'You're either walking or opening up. What is your problem?'

'I'm just a reject—I'm just like the rest of them. You're going to leave me'.

Eddie tried to point Ewan to the ultimate security—the promise that God would never leave him or forsake him. Eventually, Eddie hoped Ewan would be able to work through the deep scars that he carried.

It was not to be. As Eddie was returning from a trip to England he received a call. 'Ewan is on a life-support machine; he's overdosed and he's dying. Please come.'

Ewan had taken a cocktail of tablets and lay motionless on his bed. Eddie was very distressed.

As he bent over him he vented his frustration with an angry outburst. 'Ewan! If you don't waken up right now I'm going to kick your backside so hard that you're going to go through this wall. Waken up!' Ewan's body started to shake as he heard Eddie's voice. The nurses came running as Eddie leapt back from the bed protesting he hadn't done anything. 'Whatever you said, keep going,' said one of them, but it was too late. It was as if Ewan had been waiting for Eddie and he was saying 'Goodbye'.

Eddie took the loss hard. He loved Ewan and he had desperately wanted to help him. He felt frustrated that Ewan had made progress but had been unwilling to face the long hard road to real recovery. So much had been prepared for him—a job, and further counselling—all too late.

Ewan's death was a reminder to Eddie of the reality of the cross. Christ's death was a payment for sin for *all* those who desperately wanted new life, fresh hope and true security. Through Jesus' death on the cross, Eddie could offer *life*, even to those in hopeless situations. He longed to see people taking Christ at his word.

The Dornoch Fellowship and Aberdeen Prison

Fellowship workers who had been involved with Ewan made up an album of photographs for each of the parents. They wanted to remind them of the son that had been special to them all. The message was simple. 'You have a son to be proud of.'

Andrew was another person that Eddie met on the streets. He became friendly with both his wife and wider family. Andrew was extremely depressed and very withdrawn. He was undergoing psychiatric care but desperate for help and friendship. He had been in and out of prison, was very lonely and Eddie longed for him to find the love and friendship God offers through Jesus. But Andrew found Eddie's talk very threatening and at one point put a knife to Eddie's throat, telling him that if he heard any more he would use it. Eddie was asked to back off and give Andrew a bit of space.

It was an emotional low-spot when a week or so later Eddie got the news that Andrew had taken his own life, and was found hanging from a tree in a local park. 'Why did I back off?' Eddie asked himself. It was hard to understand how Andrew must have felt—completely overwhelmed by his inadequacy, wanting to escape from the responsibility of his wife and of his baby, which was born two months after his death.

When the family asked him to speak at the funeral service and say some 'nice things', Eddie found it all too hard. He had shared the roller-coaster feelings of the family over the months. As he walked the long road to the graveyard in the pouring rain, water running off his hair and nose, supporting Andrew's mother, he felt absolutely drained. Where were the breakthroughs? He was later to realise that the pain and hurt that he had shared with the family was what broke through in their lives and brought both wife and mother to a living faith in the Lord Jesus Christ.

It was on days like these that Eddie simply couldn't see it all 'as part of a day's work'. He often felt his own loneliness and inadequacy as he clocked up the miles. He was only one man and he felt overwhelmed by the sheer volume of problems. A typical day might include early morning travel to a prison. There would be governors to meet, Prison Fellowship teams with which to discuss issues and resolve problems, prayer meetings and Bible Studies. Then in the afternoon Eddie might meet up with a mother who couldn't cope after hearing her son was charged with murder. A Drop-In Centre session followed, then it was back to another prison for an evening meeting. The meeting over, another home support visit might follow and Eddie would arrive back home in the early hours—day after day.

Was it worth it? Definitely! Eddie knew that his Lord was faithful. Furthermore he wanted to help people and he wanted to get involved! He knew that for every Ewan and Andrew there would be others that would 'break through'.

One day, whilst at church in Aberdeen, a couple approached Eddie asking if he would consider helping the husband's brother. 'Michael has a drink problem,' they said. 'Would you agree to meeting him?'

Eddie wanted to assess Michael first, and agreed to talk to him briefly. They met and had a short discussion in Eddie's car.

Michael was very cautious. He knew Eddie was 'Church' and he was clearly assessing how much he could say.

Eddie, on the other hand, was blunt. 'I want to meet you next week, same time, same place.

If you can't be honest about the problem, where you are and where you want to be, I won't help,' he promised.

At the next meeting it still took a while before Michael could admit honestly that he had a serious drug and alcohol problem.

Eddie was so determined that he wasn't going to mess up that he came down on him hard. He wanted to lift the lid and show Michael his basic self–centredness. After two weeks Eddie got him into a rehabilitation centre. Several months later his family contacted Eddie to say that Michael was clean. His parents were very relieved and full of gratitude and Michael's successful withdrawal was an encouragement to Eddie. Despite all the seeming failures there were also positive results.

Living with the past
Nowadays Michael is a leader in a drug rehabilitation centre. Like so many who share a troubled past he finds it hard to control his feelings of regret and condemnation for what he has done.

Eddie knows those feelings all too well, but also knows they have to be dealt with. 'We've all done things that are wrong – some terrible things – and when we feel shame, remorse, regret and condemnation it can overwhelm us. But we should not accept a continual spirit of condemnation.'

Sometimes other people are responsible for reminders of the past. A year or so ago, for example, Eddie was due to lead an Encounter Weekend, where he was taking a group of people away for Bible Study. Just before it he had a phone call from a policeman. 'What right have you got to try and help people with your background and the things you have done? You should be ashamed to do what you're doing!' Eddie found it very hard. It churned him up inside. It wasn't easy to turn the conversation around and suggest the policeman think through the implications of what he was saying.

That weekend, with the conversation still fresh in his mind, Eddie had to talk about the subject of condemnation and the pain it caused. He was able to explain that conviction of sin and seeking forgiveness from God are both necessary and healthy in order to move on. He also stressed the need to say sorry to those sinned against, although rarely can the clock be turned back.

Eddie believes what the Bible teaches, that even in extreme situations Christ paid for 'the condemned' to be set free, and that he needs to discipline himself, so that his mind is not trapped by continual remorse.

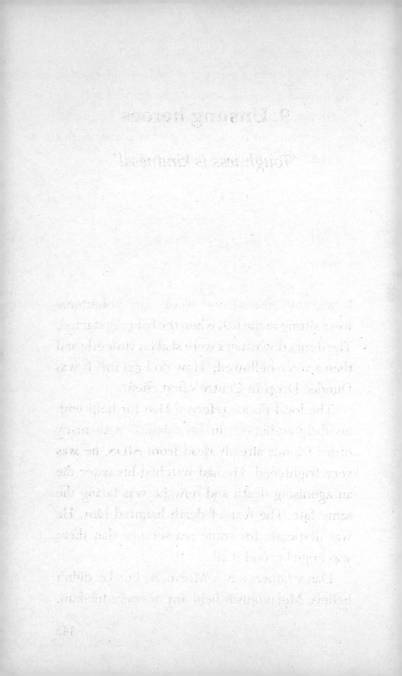

9. Unsung heroes

'Toughness is kindness!'

It was only the second week. The volunteers were sitting in the hall when the banging started. The doors downstairs were shaken violently and then a voice bellowed, 'How do I get in?' It was Dundee Drop-In Centre's first client.

The local police referred Dan for help with his drug addiction. In his thirties, with many of his friends already dead from AIDS, he was very frightened. He had watched his sister die an agonising death and now he was facing the same fate. The fear of death haunted him. He was desperate for some reassurance that there was hope beyond it all.

Dan's father was a Mormon, but he didn't believe Mormonism held any answers for him.

He turned to the Drop-In Centre for help. It was plain to the volunteers that Dan's urgent need could only be met by a relationship with the living Christ, and they began to pray for just that. As the weeks went by, people started to notice a change in Dan. His whole character softened and the hard look disappeared from his face. He began to relax as he felt the support of those around him. Prison Fellowship volunteers began to visit him at his flat to share the Gospel and to counsel and support his girlfriend, who was also doing drugs. As he opened up and talked about his fears and insecurities the team prayed for God to give healing to his mind and a living hope. The turning point was when Dan realised that the Lord Jesus Christ had conquered death by dying on the cross and taken away *his* sin and that he now had a hope and a future.

Dan is a very typical example of the complex situations that workers face in a Drop–In Centre. What are the priorities? Can anyone be prepared and trained to support such wide–ranging problems? Dundee Drop–In Centre was about to find out.

Dundee Drop-in Centre

Getting Dundee Drop-In Centre off the ground was a challenge for Eddie, and laid the foundations for future Drop-In Centres. Two trustees from Prison Fellowship found premises, a hall in Mary Slessor Church of Scotland and it was Eddie's job to establish the work. He began by inviting local churches to hear his testimony and spoke about the value of a Drop-In Centre and how it would work. Drawing from a core of interest, he established a weekly Wednesday Drop-In Centre, organising training weekends to train volunteers to counsel and to listen, to deal with very emotional and traumatic sessions, and to teach them practical issues such as preparing food and setting up the room for a session. The team quickly realised that a draughty upstairs hall with bare wooden floorboards wasn't ideal and later transferred downstairs to a cafe area that was carpeted and heated properly. It made a significant difference to the welcome feel.

The centre attracted a healthy mix of people—ex-offenders, individuals with a variety of problems, families whose lives were pulled apart by the effects of drug abuse. Some were referred by other agencies, realising that the

Drop-In could offer more structured support.

One young woman returned week after week suffering from the trauma of being gang-raped. She shared her suicidal feelings, low self–esteem and a wealth of practical problems with the volunteer team, and found the Centre to be a place of understanding and help.

Gary was an ex-offender. He barged into the Centre and thumped on the table for attention. 'Can your God do something for me? I've just finished a long stretch and I've bin sentenced again. I've got six months. I've got cancer.'

'God may not take away your cancer, but he can help you to cope with your situation,' Eddie said, and he and the staff started to pray.

Next week Gary was back and they prayed for him again. Then nothing. Gary seemed to have disappeared completely and enquiries as to his whereabouts drew a blank. Out of the blue Gary arrived with an enormous carrier bag filled with chocolate gateaux to share with the staff. 'Where have you been?' they asked. 'And where did you get these?' (searching for the till receipt!).

'You'll never believe this,' Gary said, 'but after you prayed for me something happened inside'

(He pointed to his heart). 'Such a peace came into my heart. You know something? I knew I was going to heaven,' he said, 'but I was very scared I wouldn't know anyone there. So I've been to all my family and friends and told them all about Jesus and what he's done for me.'

It was pouring with rain when Eddie got into his car, but nothing could dampen his spirits. All he could think of was his wonderful Saviour! Sometimes the Drop-In Centre was an overwhelmingly joyful place to be.

Unsung heroes

You can imagine how hard it is finding volunteers willing to tackle circumstances like these. Many see the value of the work and think they have a contribution to make, but they don't last long. Some unconsciously volunteer for the wrong reasons, using it to build up their own insecurities and rejections. The volunteers of a Drop-In Centre are very special people. The nature of their work is often deeply disturbing. They share in peoples' pain. They follow the ups and downs of peoples' lives. It is their awesome privilege to see the beauty and power of the Gospel message at work.

Most volunteers are older people. Eddie's experience is that they are 'unsung heroes'. They know what life is about and they are not afraid to be themselves. They've already notched up maturity and experience and they're not afraid to listen. Some people who arrive on the doorstep wanting help are desperate for a sense of family, and have never known a supportive and loving family before. They identify quickly with a 'granny' or 'grandpa' figure. Although Prison Fellowship employees are bound by a 'no touch' policy, volunteers are sometimes drawn to offer the love and comfort that only a hug can demonstrate. 'Some of these folk go the extra mile, give compassion and are not scared to get hurt. They see God at work,' Eddie explains. 'But it's *hard* work!'

The Dundee Drop-In Centre ran for several years and eventually closed. 'We needed to make changes and decided to re–launch in Aberdeen,' Eddie explained, 'making a new foundation from all that we'd learnt. Perth Drop-In Centre is now up and running, with plans to open a similar Centre in Inverness.

Drop-In Centres now have a very clear and proven structure. Before opening, volunteers arrive to pray and then food is prepared – usually simple sandwiches and soup – and tables are set out and laid. Once the Centre is opened people come in under Zero Tolerance rules— no drink, no drugs, no arguments, no fighting, no swearing or cursing. 'They know that no one can cause problems and that helps to make people feel secure and able to talk about their problems and,' Eddie says forcefully, 'anyone causing trouble is out on their ear and banned for a week or maybe two.'

After the meal there is a fifteen to twenty-minute worship time, followed by a simple message designed to lift people and lead them to Christ. It is followed by a time of counselling. Tea and coffee are put out on the tables, allowing a time for people to talk casually, to offload worries and problems, and further counselling is offered.

Getting people to open up and share is all–important. When God's Word is presented, the Holy Spirit uses the truth to open the mind. But building up trust and a secure environment to encourage the ongoing work is crucial. 'I would love to see all the Centres with full–time support that is 'on-call'',' Eddie says. 'When a crisis arises we need to be able to respond. That's where the need is and that's where bridges will be built.'

In Aberdeen a mother resorted to the Drop–In Centre after looking for lost coins down the back of her sofa and finding used needles instead. She had her son, Sean, and granddaughter living with her. A number of things now made sense, money missing from her purse, articles missing from the house. She realised that she could no longer trust Sean. A nightmarish scenario presented itself. What if her son had AIDS? What if her granddaughter had handled dirty needles? Why didn't Sean see he had a problem?

Eddie's reaction was tough and uncompromising, and others involved found it too hard. 'Chuck him out. Don't give him any money. When he's in the gutter make sure he's got the Drop-In Centre phone number. If he really wants help he'll come.'

He did. Within a short time Sean was in a re–habilitation centre in Edinburgh. Even though there was a struggle to come home over Christmas he stayed and persevered, and to date is clean of drugs.

Drop-In Centres often have opportunities to profoundly influence whole families and in some cases several generations come to saving faith in Christ. In Perth Drop-In Centre the counselling of a suicidal young woman whose husband had died of AIDS led to her conversion. When the young woman professed faith and asked to be baptized she was joined at the front of the church by her father and later by one of her daughters—three generations brought to faith. She testified that on one visit to the Drop-In Centre a volunteer had prayed that the spirit of suicide be broken. For the first time she had felt a flicker of hope that grew into full healing.

Occasionally volunteers themselves have problems that need dealing with. With great shame one volunteer, happily married for years and attending church Sunday by Sunday, admitted to his minister that he was 'a sleekit alcoholic'. His wider family had no idea that he drank bottles of whisky, that the Coke cans held whisky or beer and that his weekly afternoon off was spent down the pub. But his wife knew the score. The pressure came to a head when she told him that unless he dealt with the problem they were finished.

Eddie refused to play games. 'I told him that if he was willing to lose his family and his kids just for his addiction he hadn't got any bottle!' he grins. 'My job is to make people see actual reality,' he says. 'The volunteers have the job of building up and supporting. This man needed tough love and he responded. His wife tells me he's a new husband. He's also found a new faith!'

One of the inevitable frustrations of the Drop–In Centre work for Eddie was not staying in one place long enough to give significant support.

Weekends away

Weekends away gave opportunities to concentrate on issues raised in Drop-In Centre sessions.

Aberdeen Drop-In Centre organised one such weekend, taking approximately fifty people to a large house in Newtonmore. The logistics of travel and self–catering were complicated and meant pooling volunteers from several Drop-In Centres but presented a unique opportunity to get alongside people. 'The talks just seemed to break people down,' Eddie remembers. 'There were people running from the room in tears, unable to cope with subjects like rejection and insecurity. We could really feel the power of God working in peoples' lives. Even on the way back, whilst I was driving the bus, a guy shared his problems, giving us the opportunity to help him find new accommodation and a fresh start. His girlfriend came down and got a job in a Christian coffee shop. I had the privilege of marrying them a few months later. They've since moved back to Aberdeen.

Tough love

Many Christians find tough love a very difficult concept but Eddie has lived in a different world. He believes that people need to face their responsibilities and to see the reality of a situation. 'When people are alcoholics and are in danger of losing their wife and kids, they need to have their backsides kicked and face up to what they are losing. Many Christians live in a sheltered world and don't want to know the meaning of Christ's teaching about overcoming sin The guys however that have the problem – drink, drugs or sex – have no illusions about themselves when they've reached rock bottom. These guys have got to change to survive. In our society Christians have fallen into the trap of believing there is an instant and easy way out. The Christian life is about tough love. Christ's death was a demonstration of tough love. We've all got weaknesses that need overcoming. The Bible is clear that we need spiritual wisdom and understanding. One of my favourite Bible passages is Proverbs, chapter 2—it talks about how we need to wise-up to keep on the right track. The Church should be less compromising and preach tough love, but is afraid of turning people off.'

Eddie is also clear that tough love is different from criticism. He has seen at first-hand how one word out of place in prison can meet with extreme violence. Equally, Eddie has seen churches confuse discipline and criticism, and abuse position to strip a person of self–worth and cause emotional damage. Tough love is positive and honest. It seeks to restore goodness, knowledge, wisdom, love and discipline into peoples' lives.

10. Exploding point

*'Have you learnt
to confide in someone?'*

Over the period that Eddie has worked for Prison
Fellowship he has certainly got around! His first
book, *Bruised but not Broken,* has brought many
opportunities to speak and to preach, sometimes
in unexpected places. On two occasions Eddie
has been invited to appear on television. *The
Time The Place,* broadcast from Grampian's
Aberdeen studios, asked 'Does crime pay?' and
on its *Testimony* programme Eddie was featured
in a discussion on 'Conscience—nature or
nurture?'

Eddie's story often strikes a chord with
listeners and they contact him for help.
Telephone calls are the worst. Eddie often has to
think on his feet and defuse an emotional crisis

very quickly. 'It's similar to reactions needed at a road traffic accident—I'm there to stop the bleeding and to stabilise the person. I need to identify where the pain is and counteract the problem with truth and then bandage someone up with the healing of Scripture, and offer love and comfort. People need that release, but it can be exhausting.'

Counselling skills

Eddie has found training in counselling invaluable. He counts it a great blessing that someone, after hearing him speak, realised the need for him to have training and enrolled him at her personal expense. Eddie has now attended several counselling courses and is very appreciative of the skills he has learned. As Eddie has matured as a Christian he has learned to be 'transparent'. His past enables him to relate to and empathise with the world that many of his clients live in. His own past lack of self-esteem makes him determined to show his clients unconditional and positive regard. He also accepts when he is out of his depth and is quite happy to draw on other agencies, especially with problems such as sexual abuse.

Correspondence

Answering letters isn't much easier. Eddie is 'agony uncle' to all those who write to him requesting advice and help. For a man who has never found putting pen to paper easy this has been quite a challenge.

Thankfully many write to say how much they have been moved and blessed by his ministry and admit that Eddie has opened up a different world!

Other letters reveal a world of hidden sorrow. How messy some people's lives are! These are the people who turn to Eddie for help because he has lived in their world. They know that what he has been through qualifies him to understand. Sometimes the letters are hard to read, written by people unused to writing, but they have a familiar ring about them.

Wendy for example heard Eddie speak, and wrote to him explaining that she had been sexually abused over many years by her father. She wanted to know how Leslie, Eddie's wife, had coped with his background. 'Did she let you talk about it? Or did she blank it out? My ex-boyfriend never let me talk about my past and I'm hurting inside. I want to let Jesus into my life but I'm scared in case He'll use me and dump me too. What do I do?'

Successive letters tell Eddie of Wendy's ups and downs. Soon after giving her life to the Lord, Wendy writes: 'I'm sitting reading Matthew. I went down to see my mum and my dad and Anne was there. My dad he spoke to me and asked what kind of day did I have. ... I told him a good one because it is and I'm so happy I want to tell the world.'

A month later she writes, 'I'm feeling really down today—so I bought a 2L bottle of strong cider and drank the lot. I spoke to Jesus. I asked if he was listening to me and if yes to please help me. Why do this to myself? I think of my past and I'm not worth bothering about and why did my dad sexually abuse me Did I do something wrong? ... I cried the other night. Just for a short period. There's a lot more to come but I'm scared to show my emotions 'cause we're not supposed to show.'

Then she has the courage to write to her mum:

This is the hardest thing I've had to write in my life—I'm in a sanctuary just now and I'm safe. I'm also having advice and support from the police.

There is no gentle way of telling you this but you have to know. In the past I have been too terrified to tell you. Dad has been sexually abusing me since I was six and he's still doing it and making obscene phone calls. That is why I behaved the way I did when I was younger and I'm worried about Joanne and I've kept a watchful eye on her. ... I'm sorry this is going to upset you but it has to stop. I don't blame you.

Margaret wrote to Eddie about her son. Dean was nineteen years old, unemployed, in debt, smoking cannabis and rejected by the army because he had a criminal record. Aimless and fed up with life, he was desperate to get out of small town life. She asks, 'Please could you send him some encouragement that may help him to settle down?'

Eddie replies and asks Margaret if there is anyone locally that could come alongside Dean. She replies, 'I am afraid there is not. As I told you on the phone, my minister just doesn't know how to deal with a situation like this, and as for the young people in the fellowship, most of them have led quite sheltered lives and wouldn't know how to handle Dean.'

Eddie also speaks to Dean on the phone. But Margaret's next letter tells of the worsening situation. 'Dean is keeping well but still not working, he is waiting on word about an unpaid fine he has and is fully expecting to be jailed as the alternative. He also has a court appearance—he is co–accused on a number of charges. We all have to wait and see how things go. He has gone ahead and taken an interest in a job in a filling-station. It is only part time but is better than nothing.'

Dean then writes: 'I thank you for giving me some hope. Your phone call came as I was sitting going through my mind about all my debts with drugs and with old girlfriends. This is a wee letter to tell you what was going through my mind. The night before you phoned I took the worst beating for debt yet, an old girlfriend set me up after the pub. A couple of older guys put me over a wall and punched me about and messed my face up a little bit. At the time I was on about ten blues and a good drink (a mix that usually gets me in trouble) and I didn't feel much pain at the time. After screaming in my ear asking whether I was paying the lass, they left me on the wall. I got up and walked away wiping the blood off my face. An onlooker shouted "Are you alright son?" I shouted back "of course" to make the men look small but I was really scared and angry. This was the second time the same mob had arranged to get me on my own without any of my mates ... so I went to a mate's house trying to get a knife. I was going to get their main man, my enemy, but only with a couple of good words and a swift stabbing would I catch him off–guard. The guy's a big boxer and I'm a normal sized 19 year old but I've still got a reputation to keep. Revenge was set in my mind and still is but it's reducing since you phoned me and I started reading your book. It's a good story to read and gives me hope. If a man like yourself who went all the way through jails and through a lot of circumstances in life that make me laugh because they are the same as me. Like dropping people I loved for a life and drugs I couldn't do without or going into the shops and walking out with jeans and tops, breaking into places and helping myself for some reason. It's not too often I get caught ... after Christmas [I] took 5 charges out of a good possible 40 with the amount of things I have to steal when out of work. This is not the life I want. I love God and have always believed in Him. But circumstances and a weak tendency to steal and to get myself stoned are all around me. I know everybody and everybody knows me, especially shopkeepers. I just want out of it all. I pray you will pray for me, for my spirit to strengthen and for my mother not to worry as she does a lot. This hurts me as it's all my fault and there's nobody I love as much as my ma. I've never seen her as happy since you phoned and I thank you for this.'

Dean's mother keeps Eddie posted. 'We both will be very pleased if you can visit us and both look forward to further news. Dean went to court on Thursday past and was immediately arrested when he got inside the courthouse and taken down to the cells. This was for non-payment of his fine. He was eventually taken back up to the court for his part in the break–in and theft of a jacket, but as there has still not been any social work report given, his sentence has again be deferred until a later date. Twice he has had an appointment to see a social worker. The first time he went he was told the social worker was sick, and the next time the social worker was away on holiday. His next court hearing is in three weeks. I'm afraid right now he doesn't have much in life to cheer him but I still feel he has to make an effort to get his life into a better way.'

Letters sometimes come from unexpected and far flung places. Kennedy Muzata writes from a Zambian prison, imprisoned for treason and awaiting a death sentence. He writes: 'I saw a friend, a condemned prisoner as well, entering in my cell holding a small book. He gave it to me and I went through it. The message was a vital one and I was touched by the contents of this precious book entitled *Bruised but not Broken*. This was where I got your address from. I'm now a born-again Christian, a soldier of God and I write to you as a soul filled with much desire to spiritual growth as a born child desires milk of the mother for his growth (1 Pet. 2:2).

Getting our hands dirty
Eddie knows that his role as an 'Agony Uncle' is an important link for many people who feel they have nobody to turn to, and he takes it very seriously.

But he also sees how vital it is to train and equip Christians to work as a team. He is very aware that without back-up and training his initial work can not be developed. 'We're in a battle. Whoever heard of a battle plan where the troops stayed at home and the generals went to the front line? It is the generals who form the battle plan and they convey the strategy and send out the fighting force. The foot soldiers are the least experienced but they are the ones who see the action!' Eddie wants to challenge traditional church attitudes of the minister doing all the work. He firmly believes that everyone should get their hands dirty and live out their faith in a practical way. He has an unwavering belief that if we were to take it seriously the very fabric of our society would be impacted.

11. No easy way out

'When you have a problem do you always take the easy way out?'

Pauline had a drug problem from a very early age. It started in her first year in secondary school. She had toothache and her mother gave her painkillers, two white tablets.

If she had difficulty sleeping, Pauline's mother would also give her a blue tablet. The little blue and white tablets became a regular answer to Pauline's teenage ups and downs. Whatever the problem, whether it was the usual monthly pains or a fall-out with her boyfriend, Anthony, whom she met after school, her mother didn't talk but handed her a cup of tea and tablets, and ordered her off to bed.

The comforting routine continued even when, at seventeen, Pauline married Anthony—

until one day she woke up to cramping pain in her muscles and joints, and stomach pains, and realised something was badly wrong. She couldn't even remember how she'd got to her bed!

She and her mother went to the doctor. The doctor diagnosed something totally unexpected. Pauline was a drug addict, hooked on Codeine and sleeping tablets. Her immune system was seriously undermined and as her body demanded higher and higher doses she had begun to suffer withdrawal symptoms. The pills that were supposed to be for Pauline's mother's arthritis were strong alright! Once her mother had discussed Pauline's intake with the doctor he prescribed a massive dose to keep her going!

It wasn't a long-term answer, of course, and Pauline continued to be heavily into drugs. Her mother was always in the background offering sleeping tablets, and Pauline could never say 'No'. At eighteen she gave birth to her first child, Jamie Lee, and sixteen months later gave birth to David. Meanwhile her marriage was proving to be a disaster. Anthony was violent and mentally abusive and at the age of twenty-two they parted company and divorced.

The children were a major stabilising influence after Pauline's marriage ended. She then found a new partner. John had HIV through doing drugs. When Pauline told her mother that she planned to get married she was so angry and upset that she refused to have anything to do with them.

Her new husband was involved with Christians. Pauline was encouraged to go to church and pray. She tried lots of different churches and continued to pray and search for God. As John's illness progressed, the children, only primary-school-age and old beyond their years, helped their mum to nurse him until his death. Pauline was very dependant on the children. She couldn't go out on her own without their support. Often they missed playing with others to shop for 'messages' or to sit and keep their mum company. Pauline knew that if she went out on her own she would be tempted to buy more drugs. But it didn't stop her going to church on Saturday nights nor attending a Women and Children's Group. A friend from the Group helped Pauline by introducing her to the Bible and teaching her how to read it. It was during this time that Pauline found Perth

Drop-In Centre and a church in which she felt at home. After that she couldn't stay away—a hungry soul crying out to learn more about God. When she heard Eddie speak for the first time he asked if anyone would like to come forward for prayer. Pauline went forward and Eddie prayed very specifically that Pauline's suicidal feelings would be taken away.

That night, Pauline felt different, a faint flicker of hope for the future. Her happiness conveyed itself to her two daughters as they played together that evening. In the following days Pauline noticed the blackness, which seemed to be part of her, was lifting.

Nowadays she still takes a day at a time and is doing well over her drugs. She is also closer to her family and less dependent on her girls. Finding Jesus as her Lord and Saviour has had a huge impact on her wider family. Recently she and her father and daughter were baptised. It was a very special day for Pauline, knowing that family and friends would be there to see what an amazing difference God was making in her life.

Messed up by heroin

The first time Eddie met Stacey she was injecting heroin into her veins. She knew she was tearing her family to pieces but her only concern was to get money to feed her habit. She got by, pushing heroin. Her family could see her downward spiral into the depths of addiction and there was nothing they could do.

But Stacey was in God's hands. Christians were praying for her. Her own sister was crying out to God that He would not let Stacey die. One night she felt drawn to open her Bible and read the words of a passage from the Old Testament (2 Chron. 20:15-17). The words were about a battle that God told the Israelites He would fight for them. She read the verses to her husband, Graham, but they didn't seem to relate to her. That night Stacey's sister spent another night sleepless with worry.

How low can you go?

A few days later the sister was in Safeway when she got a phone call. Stacey had taken a massive overdose a few days earlier and they didn't know whether she would pull through. The passage from the Bible suddenly took on an amazing new meaning. 'The battle is not yours, but God's,' she read again. She thought, 'I know Stacey is at her lowest point, and I am not to be discouraged but to stand back and watch the salvation of the Lord!'

Meanwhile, Stacey's brother asked Eddie to go to the hospital and talk to her. It was the first afternoon Eddie had had free for months. As he sat next to her bed and spoke of his past, and how wonderfully changed he was through coming to know the Lord Jesus Christ it broke Stacey completely. 'When I looked into Eddie's face,' she remembered, 'I felt that the Lord Jesus was reflecting back at me and I knew I was dying, not humanly speaking, but in sin. I was overwhelmed with shame, guilt, sadness— every emotion you can think of.' Stacey cried like a baby. 'Lord help *me,*' she begged.

When Eddie had gone, Stacey began honestly to think through the alternatives. There weren't very many! She didn't want to go home. She wished she were dead. If, and it was a very big 'if', she put her trust in the God of miracles and allowed Him to do the transforming work that He had done in Eddie's life, she knew she could be cured.

The seed was sown and it had started to take root, but there were a lot of weeds around it. Stacey managed eight weeks 'clean'. She decided to go to a Christian re-habilitation centre in Wales. But things started to deteriorate rapidly and the downward spiral was re—established. She then started to sell her furniture—anything to get money to feed her habit. Once her belongings were gone she only had herself to sell and she roamed the streets looking for buyers.

But this time, although the heroin controlled her, Stacey wanted out. A 'clean-up' programme at Detox 5 (a private clinic that eases a client through withdrawal using heavy sedation) fell through. It was a lifeline thrown to a dying woman and to have it withdrawn was a terrible blow. Stacey was absolutely desperate.

She confided in Eddie. She was so afraid of death. She was afraid that one day she would get into a customer's car and never get out alive. She was afraid of dying with a needle in her arm and she was so ashamed.

But Stacey sank even lower. She began to steal—clothes, credit cards, social security books. It went on for weeks. Finally, she couldn't eat or sleep, couldn't speak to Mick, her boyfriend, properly and her guilt drove her to the police. There was already a warrant out for her arrest as she had breached her community service. She knew she faced a prison term.

Stacey told the police everything and faced going to court. In the courtroom craving for another fix she wondered how she would ever come clean. She needed to. She had to. Mick, her boyfriend, was sitting behind her with £80 worth of drugs in his pocket. She felt so bad. Perhaps if she pleaded illness her solicitor could get her court case deferred for a couple of hours and she could get one more hit.

She realised that the only way to come clean was to be put in prison for long enough to go through the drug reduction programme, which lasted for thirty days. The sentence was passed— thirty days, but in reality only fourteen.

Five days before her release Stacey knew this was the end of the line. She just couldn't go back to the life she was living. She cried out for God to help, but she believed that she had turned her back on Him so many times that she had no right to ask. In sheer desperation she tied a sheet around her neck, stood on a chair, tied the other end to the bars against her window, and pushed her chair away.

The next thing she knew she was lying on the prison floor surrounded by prison officers asking if she was okay. Her cell—mate had woken and raised the alarm. Stacey hated her for that. Stacey was sent to the Segregation Unit and Eddie was contacted to say that she had attempted suicide. She had two days to think things through. She had two days to think things through before her release and she was very scared.

Stacey prayed and prayed and prayed. 'Please help me. Lord, you have to help me. I don't want to be like this any more. I'm in such a mess. I don't want to go back to my husband and prostitution, but I've nowhere to go. Please give me help from doctors, councils, social workers. I've come close to dying twice and you've saved me. Please help me. Amen.'

The day of release arrived. Stacey was met by Mick and two women from Prison Fellowship. The four of them met up with Eddie. Stacey's first visit was to a doctor and her first prayer was answered—she was prescribed Methadone. Then Christians running a B&B were able to offer her short-term accommodation. This was a real answer to prayer, for it was well away from areas where heroin was hawked. The stay in the B&B was followed only a few days later by an amazing and immediate provision of a council house in a quiet street—an almost unheard of thing!

Stacey has a real sense of God at work in her life and a deep thankfulness for daily strength. The battle hasn't been completely won. Every day she has cravings for 'smack', but she believes that the victory is through her Heavenly Father's strength. With His help she will make it through.

No easy way out

Eddie is tough and often brutally truthful in dealing with addicts. He believes there is no easy way out and that people need to see themselves as they really are before they will accept help.

He doesn't believe that Methadone, for example, is a realistic option. It is, after all, still a drug and creates a greater dependency than heroin. It has the benefits of being legal and controlled, and helps to keep addicts off the streets but, at the end of the day, it isn't a total solution. Eddie would like to see counselling programmes extended so that an addict is automatically given counselling alongside a Methadone withdrawal programme. At present the demand is so high that many addicts have a two-year wait for counselling and by then their resolve to go through withdrawal has gone.

When Eddie counsels someone to withdraw from Methadone he doesn't do it lightly nor does he bypass other agencies or support mechanisms. Withdrawal is a slow, step–by–step reduction monitored by the patient's GP with referral to a psychiatrist if necessary. Eddie is notified of the client's progress by the doctor so that he knows when to progress to the next level. The whole procedure is supported by a team which often includes the person's family.

The reality is sobering. Eddie supports too many addicts who don't want to come off drugs—they want an easy way out. They prefer to hug the pain and go round and round in a 'poor me' syndrome of self-pity. How do you give someone the strength of mind and resolve to fight for themselves? The Bible says that the truth sets people free. Often addicts do need to reach rock-bottom before they accept the truth of where they are. Then the addict has to be built up emotionally, to have a sense of self-respect and to learn to take on responsibility. The Methadone option is only a small part of the story.

12. Manhattan, Bogota and the future

'Is it time to move on?'

The year 2000 marked a huge change in direction for Eddie. It started with a trip to a family in wealthy Manhattan.

Eddie was driving to Glasgow's Barlinnie Prison, accompanied by Michael Harkness, an Orcadian Christian singer, when his mobile rang. A voice with an American accent asked whether Eddie would like to come to New York for six days. Eddie decided it was a practical joke and told the unknown caller in no uncertain terms to 'stop muckin' aboot' and cut him off.

The next time the mobile rang the joker revealed himself as the Rev. Iain MacAskill, a Free Church minister from the Island of Uist! Iain asked Eddie if he would be willing to give support to a Christian family that were at the end of their tether.

He explained that a young woman had become emotionally involved with a much older man and had moved into his flat. He was working in the film industry and their daughter was drawn into his lifestyle. The parents were deeply concerned about the influence he was having on their daughter. They could see she was getting deeper and deeper into the darker side of the glitz and was dabbling in drugs. The combination of a good education, plenty of money and an insecure upbringing, in which the daughter had felt rejected, had made her a 'spoilt brat'—rebellious and defiant. Now unable to face her dilemma she had become suicidal and desperately needed help.

Her parents didn't know where to turn. Whenever they tried to talk through the issues their daughter flew into a rage and they were each at their wit's end.

It seemed unlikely that a Presbyterian minister in the Outer Hebrides should be the catalyst for help, but a 'chance' holiday meeting in Uist, and correspondence by e-mail, kept Rev. Iain MacAskill up-to-date with their concerns.

When Iain was asked if he knew of anyone who could help he immediately thought of Eddie.

So it was that Eddie and Iain found themselves on the first available flight.

Eddie quickly grasped the situation. The girl's mother had grown up in a broken and abusive background and her problems had been outworked on her daughter. The challenge for Eddie was to help work through the issues and to provide the support for mother and daughter to be able to talk, within a very short time frame.

Progress was made in the six days, and the best news of all came right at the end of their stay when Eddie had an amazing phone call.

'I've had the best education money can buy and it taught me that your religion is rubbish,' the daughter said, 'but I've also got my heart telling me that what you're saying is the truth. I want to invite Jesus into my life.' That day was a whirlwind day of prayer and praise, and building bridges between the family before they caught the plane home.

...And then to Colombia
God was at work with Eddie as well. The trip to

Manhattan signalled the beginning of change. In Scotland Eddie was struggling. The buzz he had previously felt for his job was no longer there. 'Don't be silly!' Leslie told him. 'Stop relying on your feelings!' The feelings, however, didn't go away. Not long after, he was engaged to speak at a church in Aberdeen and the weekend turned out to be very special.

As the church heard about Eddie's work and his spiritual vision they shared their vision with him—a deep desire to see whole communities turned upside down for God. 'We want you to come to Colombia and see at first hand what is happening over there,' they said. 'It will broaden your experience of what God can do.'

After thirteen hours of travel the tropical heat enveloped Eddie as he stepped from the plane to be met by armed militia. He had arrived in the drug capital of the world.

What had God to teach him here in a country so different from his own? Could he have anything to learn from a country waging a thirty-eight-year-old civil war involving rebels, a right-wing paramilitary and government with 400,000 killed in the last decade alone? Where was God in a country where the drugs trade riddled business, politics and even religion with corruption?

All about prayer

Eddie had heard about Cali, the third largest city in Colombia, with a population of nearly three million people, where Christian people had the desire to pray. As they prayed, pleaded and fasted an incredible thing happened. Gradually things began to change and people became Christians, with whole communities impacted. People in government and in business became Christians and brought 'salt and light' into their work. The drugs cartel was spectacularly smashed in a government crackdown. Occult strongholds were broken. Everyone was talking about spiritual things, and the church became a force to be reckoned with.

Eddie's visit to Bogota proved equally instructive. His friends wanted him to see at first hand how the DNA of society could be changed by spiritual awakening and a whole city permeated by the gospel.

He could see that there was powerful opposition to any force for change. A purifying spiritual wind, which drove out corruption,

injustice and hatred, wasn't good for business—
and in Colombia it isn't good for Mafia business.
The Mafia was taking the threat seriously—after
all, God was even changing Mafia members!

It was inevitable that the Mafia fought back.
There were many stories of Christians being
persecuted, or murdered. Not so very long ago
one of the pastors was driving home with his
family after the morning service. He had been
preaching on Christ overcoming death. A car
pulled up alongside. A bullet hit the pastor's
watch and ricocheted into his throat. Another
bullet ploughed into his wife's breast. There
was blood everywhere and his wife held on to
him and kept repeating, 'You can't die. God has
a purpose for you'. He remembered saying, 'I
must hang on.' The family survived. The Church
has seen tremendous growth. In Bogota whole
communities have been impacted by God at
work, giving fresh hope for the future.

Even guerillas jumped on the bandwagon
as they saw Church leaders in positions of
influence. They thought it worthwhile to kidnap
and demand enormous ransoms for their
release. One church, on getting a ransom note,
sent back the reply that the kidnappers could

keep the pastor as they knew he was in the best possible place!

It was not surprising that church in Colombia was a bit different. Going to church was a dangerous activity so a friendly greeting at the church door accompanied by elders armed with pump action shotguns or machine guns wasn't unusual! Whilst Eddie was there, an arena was hired for an evangelistic event and as the meeting commenced guerillas blew up several garages in the vicinity. It brought home to Eddie how in the midst of the most unstable environments God is at work.

Colombia was an important encouragement to Eddie! The revival atmosphere was tangible and he could see how Christians were actively caring for their community. It was having an effect.

At one meeting a young woman, through an interpreter, challenged Eddie. The young woman had been given the wisdom to pinpoint a problem. Eddie was a hands-on man. Although he had learned very much from Prison Fellowship, welling up deep inside was a sense of frustration because he was in the wrong job. She could sense that he felt he was wasting time—all the travel, the constant paperwork and the hard work to get into places where even the chaplains didn't welcome him.

It was just what All Nations Fellowship in Aberdeen wanted Eddie to hear. The rebuke seemed to hit Eddie physically. 'My heart broke and I just buckled up and burst into tears. I was sobbing so hard two puddles appeared,' he laughed. 'When people realised and tried to get alongside I just asked them, 'Stay back—I'm hurting right now. Just leave me to know what the Lord is saying.' What hurt me most was realising that I'd lost my compassion for people, and it cut me to the core. I was in a rut of being the guy with a public testimony. I needed to get back to my first love.'

Time to move on

Returning from Colombia Eddie knew it was time to move on. Prison Fellowship had been a great blessing. He had learnt so much but he knew he was being called to work in a community and that God was leading him back to old pastures. Good News Ministries and All Nations Christian Fellowship, Aberdeen subsequently invited Eddie to be an evangelist/

pastor in the city where he feels he belongs.

He knows he is back home where his roots are and that he will meet people that know his past. He looks forward to being able to say, 'If I can do it, so can you.' Fourteen years ago God gave Eddie a vision in Union Street and now God has taken him right back to where he started.

13. Taking the church back into the community

'Are you involved in building relationships?'

The visit to Colombia helped Eddie focus very clearly on his gifts and his ministry. The work he had seen in Bogota he wanted to do in Aberdeen. He had a clear vision, a pioneer spirit and a burden that would not let go of him.

Developing the work in the beginning

With the backing of All Nations Christian Fellowship, and Good News Ministries, work started in two areas of the city, Tillydrone and Northfield.

Eddie began by building relationships and visiting families with problems. He organised a 'Relationship Building' day at Cummings Park with the help of a team from Youth With a

Mission. Some four hundred people came to the park for a barbecue along with bouncy castles and other entertainment, curious to know what it was all about. Eddie was greeted with caution at first and a police check was run to establish his credentials. But once people knew his background he was welcome! Doors began to open and opportunities to get involved with the community began to multiply.

U-turn

A Friday-night help group called U-Turn was established, to deal with issues that are central to families and communities. Eddie used his counselling skills to apply Bible teaching to issues like rejection, forgiveness, bondage (lying, guilt), finances, fears, betrayal, hurt, trust and more. The group provided a safe and secure haven for a surprising range of people, professional and working class. Eddie explains, 'These problems touch people from every walk of life – everyone knows someone who has been messed up or is part of a family struggling to cope. U–turn goes back to basics and supports people and allows them to talk in a safe environment.'

'Cell' family

It wasn't long before the work had a ripple effect! For example, Eddie visited a single mother with five children in a home where teenagers were doing drugs and pushers came to collect their debts. Practical help was offered and Eddie went to the pushers to share with them the pain and hurt that *they* were causing. Some of the pressure eased and Eddie began to see changes in the home. Some of the pushers actually agreed to go to rehabilitation centres themselves! One realised enough was enough, that *he* needed to take responsibility for his own actions, and became a Christian as a result. The changes in his life resulted in his mother also becoming a Christian. It became Eddie's first 'cell' group.

Developing a group based in the home gives families the support to take on their own responsibilities and is a vital part of Eddie's work. The home is the family's safe haven—an expression of the family living in it. It is the place where changes need to start. Eddie's job is to address behaviour and attitudes and let the gospel speak into the peoples' lives. By dealing with problems in families, positive ripples spread out and affect the community.

It's not always families from 'bad' neighbourhoods—drugs have no respect for people and professional families are not immune. Recently Eddie was approached by husband and wife worried for a son who was addicted to drugs. They had even given him help to maintain his habit rather than allow him to get deeper into trouble.

They were each at their wit's end and were willing to try anything—which in this case happened to be Eddie! Within two weeks there was a change. The teenager agreed to go to a rehabilitation centre and whilst he was there became a Christian and is now on the road to recovery. His mother said, 'I can see changes in his life, physically and emotionally. He's started to think in a balanced way again … and the pressure is off us. The peace in the home is wonderful. Both my husband and I are professionals and yet we couldn't give him what he needed. We are so blessed and encouraged by this change.'

Jesus Revolution
In 2002 a major outreach to the city of Aberdeen was conceived. All sorts of creative ideas were

suggested, including building an Xtreme skate park—the largest in Scotland! Once the idea was off the drawing board and the building work started, Eddie was in his element. All his practical skills were put to good use and he worked all hours, arriving home bruised, battered and absolutely filthy.

The skate park has since been officially recognised and supported by local initiatives, who see the desire to promote a drug–free environment. The skate park is opened every morning with prayer and there are clear rules about language and behaviour. 'You can't swear here!' one of the guys says to a new skate boarder.

A thirty-five-strong team of Americans arrived to help and found themselves in the community on their knees, not praying but weeding gardens and giving the neighbourhood a face lift! Where opportunities presented themselves they would also help in homes where individuals were really struggling. 'Just tidying a home where someone is old and poor-sighted can be such a help,' says Eddie. 'When our bus arrived with the team on board each home was proud to offer their facilities!'

When people wanted to know, 'Why this interest in our neighbourhood?' the team would explain that the Church wanted to serve the community. They hadn't come to preach *at* people but to earn the right to share Jesus Christ with them. Their message came with actions! 'It's not a new message,' Eddie says confidently, 'it's as old as the New Testament Church! Of course there's a balance. The Bible studies need to happen too but the relationships with people have to be earned before people will listen— then a church can be established with careful and broad leadership. Many people think that council estates have got strong community spirit but the truth is that problems have got so invasive. It doesn't help that houses are too often built like army barracks with concrete play areas.'

During the Jesus Revolution Eddie and the team toured many Aberdeen communities using a bus. They would arrive at a park or play area with music blaring and Eddie would jump off the bus in his kilt with face painted with the Scottish flag yelling 'Freedom!' and give out sweets, organise football and other activities. That way they built relationships with the local children and with their parents.

In one area mothers thanked Eddie for creating security on the playground—for the first time they hadn't been anxious for the safety of their children. They told Eddie about a small gang of teenagers who were terrorising the area and how one sixteen year-old had thrown a five year-old down a flight of steps and broken his collar bone, and how they went around looking for trouble and smashing out windows in the area.

'Who are they?' Eddie asked. Before too long Eddie had the opportunity to invite the five down to the skate park and has begun work to turn these teenagers into a positive force for good in their community. A camping holiday is planned and Eddie is working on demonstrating that it is fun to be normal, and a wonderful thing to be human and even go to church!

In one area a large number of young people were hanging out, many smoking pot. As they organised activities Eddie noticed a lonely figure picking her way gingerly through the groups of young people. The woman was in her fifties and holding a shopping bag, a scarf tucked around her head. She looked like a frightened shadow ready to run at the first opportunity.

Eddie's heart went out to her. He immediately went and introduced himself. 'Hi, my name's Eddie. What's yours?' 'Sheila,' she said. Eddie was economic with words and went straight to the point! 'I know you're lonely and frightened,' he said, 'but I've got a word from God for you— He's got something for you.'

The instant he said it, the floodgates opened and she poured out her sorrows. She had no friends, no–one to share with and her mother had died two weeks before. Eddie held her as she cried like a baby and his heart ached as she told him about her hurts, her fears and her loneliness. With children milling around her she gave her heart to the Lord Jesus Christ. Eddie told her about the new family she now belonged to and the help and support they could be to her.

This is the ministry that Eddie especially enjoys. 'I love people,' he says. 'I will scan a crowd and spot an unhappy anxious face and will have to go and talk to them.'

The finale of the Jesus Revolution was a Family Day in the park with free food, games, bouncy castle, sumo-wrestling and other activities. Three buses ferried different communities to the event and there were all sorts of opportunities as a result.

Jack, for example, one of the Americans on the team, approached a group of five women. One was smoking pot and had two little children in a pram. Jack introduced himself and said he was from the church and the woman laughed in his face and sneered, 'Church is pathetic— what's church?' Several days later the group were having a Bible study in her home!

Many people gave their lives to Christ during this campaign including Eddie's future sister-in-law, her two children, her mother and a niece, three generations in all!

Nowadays, Eddie is well known in the communites he works with. 'You're trying to do something good in our community, ent ya?' the children ask. Adults reassure him, 'This is what we really need.' Eddie is getting steady referrals from the Social Work Department and homeless organisations, doctors and police. It is not the first time, for example, the Social Work Department have given him the challenge of teaching a young mother (in twelve weeks!) how to take on responsibility for her child in order to avoid fostering.

Local GPs have also requested meetings because they want to know why Eddie is seeing so many breakthroughs. Eddie is very clear that big and complex problems need big solutions and a bigger network of support. He teams Rehabilitation Centres, support units, doctors, psychiatrists, and other counsellors together to tackle problems in a far more practical way than conventional help can offer. Professional help, for example, may be backed up by practical provision. Accommodation can be organised in a secure home environment—where a damaged person is loved and accepted. Where there are appointments with counsellors and psychiatrists the person will have someone to keep them company—small practical demonstrations which provide the backdrop to professional care.

Somebody cares

Sometimes it is hard to know where to start to make a much–needed difference. Often Eddie is called to homes where wallpaper curls from the walls and the carpets are stained with filth. It was obvious that there is little income and a struggle to maintain the home.

Gifts such as a vacuum cleaner and a tumble dryer meet with profound gratitude, but through the tears other problems are revealed—income being drained into the pockets of a drug addicted son, no resources to meet children's clothes for the new term, nor even money for the gas meter.

The challenge of entering a home like this and starting to make differences isn't just about giving money but educating the family to take on its own responsibilities. 'No gain without pain,' Eddie counsels as he works out an action plan which will detail the way forward.

Just recently, Eddie was referred to a lady in her sixties. Confused and lonely, and living in appalling conditions, she needed immediate attention. Social Services were notified. Eddie and a team of volunteers stripped her house—removing furniture and bedding which were moving with lice. A Stonehaven ministry called The Net delivered good condition second-hand furniture free of charge. The kitchen was fitted with a new microwave and fridge. The lady didn't even have cutlery! A support system is now being organised with the help of her family and volunteers to provide companionship and prevent the grandchildren (who are drug addicts) from wrecking and removing furniture in the future.

Sometimes there are people who social workers and doctors feel they cannot treat and are referred. Recently a young man took his girlfriend's supply of Methadone in order to save the life of their unborn baby, overdosed and died. The baby has since died and the woman is overwhelmed by guilt. She has resorted to Tarot cards and the occult in her desperation for spiritual peace.

Pioneering spirit?

It is easy for some people to view Eddie as arrogant. He describes himself as having 'tunnel vision' which sometimes doesn't endear itself to others. 'Breaking new ground will always reveal insecurities in people especially if there are results,' he says. 'And sometimes I do need to be reined in and reminded I am part of a team and accountable. I know I am the hammer, though,' he laughs. 'The troops move in behind me!'

Since starting to work alongside people in Aberdeen, in their homes and in their communities, Eddie is even more convinced of the need to challenge the traditional mindset of Christians and ask them to be involved in peoples' lives, not simply in bringing them to church.

'The days of just bringing people to church are finished,' Eddie reckons. 'We need to get alongside people and touch them at 'door level'. We need to prove to people that the Church can relate to them. We need to build relationships that earn us the right to talk about Jesus … and that's hard because the Church is predominantly middle class.'

14. Postscript

I have been a Christian now coming on eighteen years. It's been a long hard road at times but God has been faithful, and walked the road with me.

Leslie and I have been married for fifteen years and God has blessed us with three lovely children. What God has put together let no man separate.

I have a long road still to travel but I rejoice that the Lord is worth loving and I have a life worth living.

My life seems to be summed up in that beautiful verse—Jesus is the Way, the Truth and the Life.

In prison I found Jesus to be The Way to life

through his death on the cross—it felt as though it was just for me. And I know that He rose on the third day triumphant over death and has dealt once and for all for my sin.

I have also discovered that He is Truth. In coming to know Jesus I have had to face up to the truth about myself. Jesus has shown me the way to live is by His truth—my life coming into alignment with His Word, the Bible. In fact, it is as I fell in love with Jesus that it has been easy to follow him.

I can honestly say that Jesus has become my Life. He is my security and my protection from trouble and He leads me and teaches me the way I should go (Ps. 32:7-8).Maybe you are looking for something to give you meaning in your life and you would love to have a spring back in your step. Look to the cross.There you will see the crossroads you face—choose life, choose Jesus.

Eddie Murison
December 2004

15. Help!

...with substance addiction

Bethany Christian Centre, 6 Casselbank Street, Edinburgh, EH6 5HA, offers residential service for men with substance abuse problems; provides aftercare, pre–employment training, long-term housing. Tel. 0131 554 4071

Teen Challenge UK, 52 Penygroes Road, Gorslas, Llanelli, SA14 7LA, has nineteen residential centres for people with addiction problems and provides evangelism outreach on streets, in schools and churches. Tel. 01269 842 718

... with alcoholism—The Twelve Steps
Alcoholics Anonymous, P.O. Box 1, Stonebow House, Stonebow, York, YO1 7NJ. Tel. 01904 644 026
www.alcoholics–anonymous.org.uk

... with marriage and families
Care for the Family, Garth House, Leon Avenue, Cardiff, CF4 7RG. Tel. 01229 585 974

... with the Christian faith
Alpha Course, Holy Trinity Church, Brompton Road, London, SW7 1JA, offers a fifteen-session, ten-week practical introduction to the Christian faith, primarily for non-church goers. Multicultural. Courses throughout the UK. Tel. 0171 581 8255

... with Christian discipleship and healing
Ellel Scotland, Blairmore House, Glass, Huntly, Aberdeenshire, AB54, 4XH. Tel. 01466 799 102
Ellel Ministries International, Ellel, Lancaster, LA2 0HN. Tel. 01524 751 651

...with prison

Prison Fellowship England and Wales, PO Box 945, Maldon, CM9 4EW, enables and equips volunteers in ministry to prisoners, ex–prisoners and their families. Tel. 01621 843 232

Prison Fellowship Scotland, 101 Ellesmere Street, Glasgow, G22 5QS, supports chaplains in serving the needs of prisoners, ex–prisoners and their families. Tel. 0141 332 8870

P. S.

If any reader wishes to contact Eddie Murison, then please send for details to Christian Focus Publications, Geanies House, Fearn, Ross-shire, IV20, 1TW, Scotland

Christian Focus Publications

publishes books for all ages

Our mission statement –

STAYING FAITHFUL

In dependence upon God we seek to help make His infallible Word, the Bible, relevant. Our aim is to ensure that the Lord Jesus Christ is presented as the only hope to obtain forgiveness of sin, live a useful life and look forward to heaven with Him.

REACHING OUT

Christ's last command requires us to reach out to our world with His gospel. We seek to help fulfill that by publishing books that point people towards Jesus and help them develop a Christ-like maturity. We aim to equip all levels of readers for life, work, ministry and mission.

Books in our adult range are published in three imprints.

Christian Focus contains popular works including biographies, commentaries, basic doctrine and Christian living. Our children's books are also published in this imprint.

Mentor focuses on books written at a level suitable for Bible College and seminary students, pastors, and other serious readers. The imprint includes commentaries, doctrinal studies, examination of current issues and church history.

Christian Heritage contains classic writings from the past.

Christian Focus Publications, Ltd
Geanies House, Fearn,
Ross-shire, IV20 1TW, Scotland.

info@christianfocus.com